Equipping the Saints

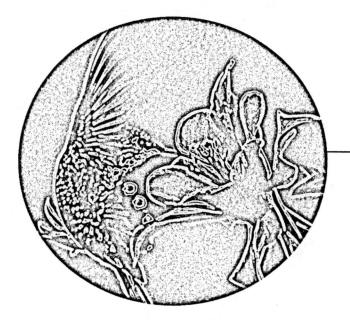

Other books by Sara Covin Juengst
from Westminster John Knox Press

Breaking Bread:
The Spiritual Significance of Food

Like a Garden:
A Biblical Spirituality of Growth

Sharing Faith with Children:
Rethinking the Children's Sermon

EQUIPPING THE SAINTS

Teacher Training in the Church

Sara Covin Juengst

Westminster John Knox Press
Louisville, Kentucky

Scripture quotations, unless otherwise noted, are from the New Revised Standard Version of the Bible, copyright © 1989 by the Division of Christian Education of the National Council of the Churches of Christ in the U.S.A., and are used by permission.

The material in the Appendixes may be reproduced at no charge for specific use in the church.

Book and cover design by Jennifer K. Cox
Cover photo by Snaford/Agliolo. Courtesy of The Stock Market.

First edition
Published by Westminster John Knox Press
Louisville, Kentucky

This book is printed on acid-free paper that meets the American National Standards Institute Z39.48 standard. ☻

PRINTED IN THE UNITED STATES OF AMERICA
99 00 01 02 03 04 05 06 07 — 10 9 8 7 6 5 4 3 2

Library of Congress Cataloging-in-Publication Data
Juengst, Sara Covin.
  Equipping the saints : teacher training in the church / Sara Covin Juengst. — 1st ed.
    p.   cm.
  Includes bibliographical references.
  ISBN 0-664-25754-2
  1. Christian education—Teacher training.   I. Title.
  BV1533.J84   1998
  268′ .3—dc21   98-6849

To the Reverend Joe Auten
and the good folk of Lakeside Presbyterian Church, Richmond, Virginia,
who helped me plant the seeds from which this book grew

Contents

Preface

This book is a challenge to all who love "the old, old stories" of the church and want to see them passed on from generation to generation. It is a challenge that comes out of my regretful conclusion that although the church does many things well, it has neglected one of its primary tasks: equipping the saints for the work of ministry. I am especially concerned about its neglect of those saints who have been called to the important task of "traditioning" the faith, of passing on those old, old stories.

I believe it is time that we reclaim the doctrine of the priesthood of believers, restore a sense of call to the ministry of teaching, and accept the responsibility of serious preparation for those who receive this call. It is time to get the horse before the cart; to stop talking about "recruiting volunteers" and focus on "vocation"; to energize, excite, and educate the saints who have heard God's call and are willing to commit themselves to it.

My sense of urgency is shared by many of my colleagues in Christian education. I am grateful to them for encouraging me in this task. In particular, I thank those educators who have read all or parts of the manuscript and have made helpful suggestions: Don Griggs, Mary Morrison, Jocelyn Hill, Jim Davidson, Candy Reid, and Carl Lauer. I am also grateful to Oscar Hussel for his helpful insights on trends in Christian education. I cannot express enough gratitude to my editor, Stephanie Egnotovich, who has helped shape this manuscript by her thorough and careful editing. Special thanks go to my husband, Dan, without whose helpful suggestions, patient support, and computer-crisis rescues this manuscript would never have come into being.

SCJ
Willington, S.C.

Introduction:
The Challenge before Us

Some years ago, while serving as an educator on the staff of a large urban church, I met with a group of Sunday school teachers to help them plan for the coming quarter's lessons. At a pause in the conversation, Emmie, one of the teachers whom I regarded as a "pillar of the church," said thoughtfully, "You know, I'm not sure I should be teaching Sunday school, because I really don't know what I think about Jesus. He's not very real to me; he's just a man in a long, white robe who lived a long time ago."

I was stunned—not because what Emmie said was so unusual; she's not the only person who has taught Sunday school or circle Bible studies who has had questions about his or her own faith experience. What was unusual was that it was the first time in my years of experience as a church educator that I had heard a teacher openly voice uncertainties about personal faith and biblical knowledge. For the most part, those who are asked to teach are embarrassed to admit that they have questions. "If you doubt, don't tell" is the tacit understanding. But the reality is that many lay teachers in the church, like Emmie, feel ill prepared for the task they have been given.

The incident brought home to me in a vivid way that although we in the Protestant churches have stressed the doctrine of the priesthood of believers, for the most part we have done a hopelessly inadequate job of equipping that priesthood. We have failed to provide teachers and leaders in the church with an understanding of the basic rudiments of biblical knowledge and Christian theology before they teach. Instead, we have consistently put the cart before the horse by thrusting them into service without any preparation at all.

It is ironic that although we have insisted that our ministers have a thorough seminary education, we have permitted and even encouraged laypersons such as Emmie to teach with a woefully shaky foundation.

It is now clearly evident that many of the mainline churches are gasping for breath. Membership is declining; congregations are "grayer and grayer" as young adults drift away; and Sunday schools are weak in spite of splashy, new denominational resources and curricula that flourish and fall in a few years' span.

At the end of his book *A Teachable Spirit*, Richard Osmer, professor of Christian education at Princeton Theological Seminary, says:

> Mainline Protestantism is at a crossroads. The path it chooses to travel today will be of great consequence well into the next century. Its continued diminishment cannot help but diminish the whole of American life. The challenges before it are great, to be sure.

Osmer goes on to say that the challenges facing mainline Protestant churches are at the same time opportunities, chances to "become clearer about their religious identities and the normative beliefs and practices that sustain these identities."[1]

I have been a professional educator in the church for nearly fifty years. Over these five decades, I have witnessed Protestant congregations becoming ever less sure of what Osmer calls their "religious identities" and "normative beliefs and practices." We do not know who we are or what we believe. Adult Sunday school classes turn to secular books of inspirational thoughts, such as *Chicken Soup for the Soul*, rather than to God's Word.

The result of this deviation from biblical and theological source materials is an almost unbelievable religious illiteracy, even among regular churchgoers. In 1990 the Search Institute conducted a study of the effectiveness of Christian education in six mainline denominations: the Christian Church (Disciples of Christ), the Evangelical Lutheran Church in America, the Presbyterian Church (U.S.A.), the United Church of Christ, the United Methodist Church, and the Southern Baptist Convention. Among other findings, the institute's investigation revealed that although 77 percent of the persons interviewed want to learn more about the Bible, 66 percent of those interviewed do not read the Bible when alone; 51 percent read other religious materials (magazines, books, etc.) once a month or less; and 42 percent never or rarely talked about the work of God in their lives.[2]

I am convinced that one of the major reasons for our loss of religious identity, biblical illiteracy, and inarticulateness about the experience of faith is the hopelessly inadequate job most Protestant churches have done in the training and preparation of people like Emmie. The Search Institute's study revealed that an average of only 21 percent of the Sunday school teachers of the six denominations examined were given annual or more frequent instruction in denominational theology and tradition.

"Putting the cart before the horse," that is, asking people to teach before giving them adequate training, has resulted in such a weak transmittal of the faith that many of those who have been teaching Sunday school for years still are not sure, for example, which came first, Jacob or Joseph; and few can explain clearly what any one of Paul's epistles is about. We have yielded, time after time, to the expediency of drafting just "any available warm bodies" as teachers in the educational programs of the church, before they have any sort of training at all.

We have justified this practice in a variety of ways:

> We have claimed that "the best way to learn is to teach".
>
> We have insisted that a good way to make people active in the church is by giving them teaching responsibilities.
>
> We have argued that the Sunday School needs "new blood" in its teaching staff.
>
> We have believed that if we require people to get training, we'll never have enough teachers.

While each of these arguments may contain a grain of truth, they are all seriously flawed as reasons for encouraging people to teach before they have a competent grasp of what they are teaching. In fact, these justifications are dangerous and theologically irresponsible. They embody a careless attitude toward the seriousness of the teacher's task in strengthening and building up (Paul's word: edifying) the church as the body of Christ.

Lyle Schaller, an expert on what makes churches tick, believes such arguments are contributing factors toward what he terms a "passive church." He says:

> [an] excessive degree of passivity tends to be found in those congregations in which (a) there is a lack of a consistent and continuing emphasis on opportunities for personal and spiritual growth for adults, (b) there is a comparatively low level of competence in the members, and especially the leaders, in articulating their faith (this characteristic often is reinforced by the lack of any programmatic emphasis to help people develop this ability), (c) there is a conspicuous lack of any systematic and continuing program of lay leadership development, (d) there are relatively few large group fellowship and social events designed to decrease the level of anonymity among the members, and (e) almost the entire responsibility for the evangelistic outreach of the congregation and for the operation of the new member recruitment system has been delegated to paid staff members.[3]

INTRODUCTION

LOOKING BACKWARD

Although the crisis in teacher training has now reached critical proportions, discerning educators raised a warning alarm years ago. It is fascinating to look back at what has happened since then.

As early as 1954, James D. Smart, who had served for six years as editor of a new curriculum for The United Presbyterian Church in the U.S.A., stated in his classic book *The Teaching Ministry of the Church* :

> The Church as a whole has failed to take education seriously as one of its functions and to interest itself in providing the best possible system of education. Men and women, members of the church, who in their community demand that their children receive the benefits of every advance in educational theory, technique, literature, and equipment, will allow the church school to limp along little different from what it was a generation earlier.[4]

What a heartbreaking announcement from a person whose whole life had been dedicated to a belief in the importance of education! And what a tragedy that the same announcement can be made today!

Perhaps one of the contributing factors to this educational crisis, both then and now, is that many professional theologians in our Protestant seminaries have been largely indifferent to what happens in Sunday schools, as if they are beneath their notice. Few seminaries provide adequate instruction in Christian education, particularly in the basics of teacher training and leadership education. I have heard such courses disparagingly referred to as "macramé" or "light stuff," compared to the "heavier" biblical and theological courses. The result is that many seminary graduates have little or no idea of how to go about equipping the saints to do ministry, although they may feel well equipped themselves to preach, counsel, and administer the church's programs.

The reality is that the quality of the educational program in any school is determined largely by the quality of the teaching staff. Public schools know this and insist on certification and evaluations. Community agencies know this and require that volunteers receive adequate preparation for their duties, as well as good supervision. I have observed that when churches demand similar preparation for their educational programs and offer opportunities for thorough training to equip teachers, people are much more eager to teach than when no such training is provided.

At the end of Smart's book, he issued a call for more thorough training of church teachers in Bible, history, and doctrine—and his voice was heard. The 1950s and early 1960s saw a surge of interest throughout Protestant churches in the perennial problem of how to improve the quality of teaching in the church. Workers' conferences, laboratory schools, and leadership training conferences proliferated. Many seasoned educators today look back on this time as a golden age of leadership development and long for similar interest today. Something was happening.

By the late 1960s, the passion began to wane as circumstances changed—within the church as well as outside it. New denominational curricula were being developed, and the emphasis was on how to teach these materials rather than on general leadership training. A major ecumenical curriculum, *Christian Education: Shared Approaches,* contained almost no mention of teacher training, because the supporting denominations simply were not interested in funding such pieces. The rise of interest in social action concerns such as peace-making, hunger, and gender issues drained a lot of energy and funding from denominational staff and resources. Professional educators were interested more in pursuing the role of education in global awareness, ministry in the workplace, and spirituality than in training teachers to teach. The teacher manuals that accompanied curriculum pieces emphasized planning for teaching rather than equipping teachers in the basics of biblical knowledge, theology, and principles of good teaching. Even the emphasis on "self-directed learning" seemed to suggest that teachers did not need to know a lot of facts; they just needed to be skilled in helping others discover truths for themselves.

By the mid-1970s, only a few voices continued to champion the cause of teacher training, among them Donald Griggs and Locke Bowman. Their emphasis, however, was primarily on the techniques of good teaching, rather than on how to provide long-range recruitment and training programs.

The perennial problem did not go away, and in 1986, more than thirty years after Smart's 1954 cry of alarm, Bowman wrote:

> Few churches reach the ideal of thorough teacher training for everyone who works in the Sunday school. Recruiting practices vary widely. Some congregations seek only qualified teachers willing to give time and effort to their tasks commensurate with the high calling of communicating the Christian faith, while others appear to "take anyone they can get" for the Sunday school teaching staff.[5]

THE MINISTER'S ROLE

One of the serious issues that emerges in the cart-horse dilemma is the role of the minister. Although most ministers are clear about their responsibility to use the theology they learned in seminary in their own preaching and teaching, all too often they have not taken seriously their responsibility to educate Sunday school teachers systematically in theological matters. They have not given priority to providing laypersons with the tools they need to interpret and understand scripture. As a result, an enormous gap separates the clergy's level of theological understanding and that of the laity.

The tragedy is that this gap causes the body of Christ to suffer. One cannot read Ephesians without being impressed that the purpose of the various ministries performed by apostles, prophets, evangelists, and pastor-teachers is "to equip the saints for the work of ministry" (Eph. 4:12). In a curious inversion, we have concentrated on equipping not the saints but the apostles, prophets, evangelists, pastors, and professional teachers. We have come to believe that *they* are the ones who are to do ministry on behalf of the rest of us, "the saints."

As a church educator, I have discovered that in those churches where the minister is enthusiastic about a program for teacher training—planning for it, endorsing it, and actively participating in it—that program grows and flourishes. Ministers can provide expertise, enthusiasm, and encouragement. They can share biblical scholarship, theological clarification, and an understanding of what is now known about teaching and learning, growth and development. They can provide spiritual direction and guidance for lay leaders. They can be intimately involved in developing an ongoing strategy for leadership development and in the resulting process of identifying, recruiting, training, and supporting leaders. I support Elton Trueblood's belief that "lay persons are not assistants to pastors, to help them do their work. Rather, pastors are to be their assistants; they are to help equip them for the ministry to which God has called them."[6]

The importance of the minister's role in empowering the laity cannot be overestimated. If ministers were to take this task seriously, treating it as a top priority, then the church's entire educational program could be strengthened and renewed.

The question is, How do they go about "empowering the laity"? The hard, cold reality is that after forty years of talking about the problem, Protestant churches today are, for the most part, still providing little in the way of long-range recruitment and training programs in biblical instruction, basic Christian theology, and principles of good teaching and learning. Instead, we downplay the seriousness of the teaching task in order not to discourage the "warm bodies" we are trying desperately to recruit. The perennial problem is still very real. The cart is still in front of the horse.

A PROPOSED SOLUTION

In the rest of this book, I offer a year-long process of teacher training that I have tested in four congregations. The results have been extremely positive. In one church with a membership of fewer than three hundred, twelve people completed the course and became valuable teachers. In a larger church, which is field-testing the process at this writing, fifty persons signed up for the opening segment.

The heart of the process is a nine-month teacher training course, offering segments in biblical background, basic beliefs, and teaching techniques. Each segment contains thirteen sessions (three months of weekly sessions) of interactive study. All parts of the process are important. The crucial nature of the preliminary phases of thoughtful recruitment and prayerful enlistment cannot be minimized. Equally essential are the apprenticeship phase and the ongoing support and recognition provided by pastor and congregation. The vitality of the process depends on the enthusiasm and energy of those behind it: pastors, governing bodies, Christian education committees, Sunday school superintendents, and the special task force that guides the process. The various segments of the program can be used for church officer training, new member orientation, and adult elective courses as well as for teacher training. The most rewarding outcomes, however, have been the renewed enthusiasm and energy infused into tired Sunday schools and the genuine excitement and eagerness of those who completed the process.

I am convinced that a course such as this, taught by well-trained teachers using the best educational methods and offered on a regular basis, can provide an answer to the perennial problem of securing quality teachers for our church's educational work. The program stresses call and commitment rather than desperation and duty.

In chapter 1, I provide a biblical foundation for the program by reflecting on the role of teaching in scripture and Christian tradition. These reflections could provide the basis for a series of sermons in a church planning to use the program or could serve as preliminary study material for the task force charged with the responsibility for the program.

Chapter 2 examines the importance of recapturing a "theology of vocation," in which service in the church is seen as a call from God, not a burdensome duty. In this chapter I describe the first phase of the program: a detailed plan for the recruitment and enlistment of those who will participate in the program.

In chapter 3, I present lesson plans for the nine-month teacher training class's first segment, "Basic Biblical Background." This is a thirteen-session biblical overview that can also be offered as an adult elective class to anyone interested. The lesson plans include suggestions for homework, a step-by-step procedure for teaching the sessions, and a list of resources. The number of steps may exceed your time slot allowed; if this is the case, choose those steps that best suit your group.

Chapter 4 outlines the second segment, "Foundations for Faith," which encompasses the basic doctrines of the Christian faith in thirteen sessions. It also includes homework suggestions, methods for teaching and recommended resources.

Chapter 5 presents the third segment, "Timely Teaching Techniques," thirteen sessions on understanding how to use various teaching methods by participatory learning. Resources, methods, and homework are suggested.

Chapter 6 outlines the final phases of the teacher training process: apprenticeship, evaluation, and methods of support and appreciation for those who have offered their gifts in the teaching ministry of the church.

I know what you are thinking. I recognize that this process is demanding and rigorous. I acknowledge that to succeed, it will need careful planning, commitment, and enthusiastic support from clergy and other key leaders in the congregation. I am aware of the lethargy and apathy that will have to be overcome in some situations before you can even launch this process. One educator asked me, "Will people commit to such time-consuming study?"

My answer to that is "Yes, they will!" And they will be grateful you asked them to make that commitment. The evidence is already in: hundreds of people have made even longer commitments to serious Bible study in such programs as Bethel Bible Study and the Kerygma Program and have experienced the fulfillment such commitment brings. Perhaps the problem is that we don't ask enough of people, as if we ourselves are not convinced of the importance of serious commitment.

I believe in this approach because I have seen it work. I also believe in it because what is at stake may be the survival of our faith. In this "crossroads time," it is increasingly urgent that churches get the horse before the cart and begin to take seriously that important scriptural command to "equip the saints for the work of ministry" (Eph. 4:12).

1.

The Importance of Traditioning

In recent years, educators have frequently discussed the concept of "traditioning," or re-presenting ideas and customs from one generation to the next. Through traditioning, the meaning of a community is appropriated and passed on so that future members of the community will understand who they are and what it means to be a part of the community. In *The Creative Word: Canon as a Model for Biblical Education* (Philadelphia: Fortress Press, 1982), biblical scholar Walter Brueggemann calls it "the binding of the generations," the rich and unique inheritance that makes members of communities, cultures, or religious groups feel connected. Personally, when I read that my Huguenot ancestors were noted for their "zeal in the cause of education and learning," I felt a bond with them.[1]

Traditioning both *binds* and *reminds*. It binds us by providing a language through which we can claim our past, our heritage, and identify who we are in the present. It reminds us that we are not alone, that we are part of a larger community of those who share the same traditions. Well-known religious educator Maria Harris has observed that tradition is "the process by which humans communicate *ways* of knowing, *ways* of being, and *ways* of doing from one generation to the next. . . . Tradition brings together past and present, just as memory does."[2]

Why is traditioning important for the Christian community? What is the story we must re-present from generation to generation? What is it that binds us together as Christians? Of what are we to be reminded through the process of traditioning?

I have found the work of Thomas Groome very helpful in providing answers to these questions. Groome describes a pattern of learning that involves reflecting on one's own story in the light of the Christian community's story and the response which that story invites. By the Christian community's story he means the whole faith tradition of our people, however that is expressed or embodied in "particular roles and expected life-styles, written scriptures, interpretations, pious practices, sacraments, symbols, rituals, feast days, communal structures, artifacts, 'holy' places . . . which embody, express, or re-create some part of the history of that covenant." He uses "Story" as a metaphor for all these expressions of the faith tradition and declares that there is little more a Christian community can do than "authentically re-*present* its Story."[3]

Groome is right: Traditioning is necessary for the survival of any institution. The fundamental ideals and purposes of the institution must be not only understood clearly but also passed on to each succeeding generation. The implication for the church is clear: If the church is to survive, it must do a better job of equipping its teachers for the task of traditioning, that is, of re-presenting the story, of passing on to succeeding generations its fundamental ideals and purposes, its ways of knowing, ways of being, and ways of doing.

THE OLD TESTAMENT AND TRADITIONING

Traditioning is done largely through the telling of family stories. The family story for those of us in the Christian community is, without question, the biblical story. It is in the Bible that we find the foundation of our meaning and the context by which we know who we are. It is there we find our family stories.

Telling and retelling these family stories is the urgent business of our teaching ministry. Through the stories, we gain a perspective on our heritage as the people of God that illuminates our lives today and expands our sense of who we are. The task of telling and retelling is a precious and heavy responsibility. It requires knowledge of both the biblical story and how to interpret it. It requires skill in storytelling and good communication techniques. It demands sympathetic understanding of both the biblical context and the context in which the learners live.

James Fowler, professor of Theology and Human Development at Emory University, identifies the ability to understand the meaning of our experiences through stories as a significant step in faith development. This ability emerges, he claims, about age seven or eight, and "this capacity for and interest in narrative makes the school-age child particularly attentive to the stories that conserve the origins and formative experience of the familial and communal groups to which he or she belongs."[4]

The Hebrews clearly understood this. They knew how important it was to bind the generations and remind the community of its identity by recounting the mighty acts of God. They understood these acts as formative experiences—not just memories of the past but also testimonies to the liberating and sustaining power of God in the present. Deuteronomy 6:20–25 illustrates this belief:

> When your children ask you in time to come, "What is the meaning of the decrees and the statutes and the ordinances that the LORD our God has commanded you?" then you shall say to your children, "We were Pharaoh's slaves in Egypt, but the LORD brought us out of Egypt with a mighty hand. The LORD displayed before our eyes great and awesome signs and wonders against Egypt, against Pharaoh and all his household. He brought us out from there in order to bring us in, to give us the land that he promised on oath to our ancestors. Then the LORD commanded us to observe all these statutes, to fear the LORD our God, for our lasting good, so as to keep us alive, as is now the case. If we diligently observe this entire commandment before the LORD our God, as he has commanded us, we will be in the right."

In fact, throughout the book of Deuteronomy the importance of traditioning is quite clear. Old Testament scholar Patrick Miller says, "Deuteronomy as a book of instruction is concerned about instruction—its necessity, its processes, its aims, and its results. It is concerned about learning (4:10b) and teaching (4:9–10)."[5]

The meaning of the story that makes us, in part, who we are is found in Deuteronomy both in narratives and in the rules and regulations, the social and religious practices, and the signs and symbols of the tradition. These are some of the "ways of being and doing" of which Maria Harris speaks.

The instructions about the first great commandment (the Shema of Deut. 6:4–5) are a case in point. To give these words primary place, the people of God are to implant them in their hearts, keep them in their minds, make them part of their very beings. The Shema describes a relationship that shapes who the people of God are in their homes, their families, and their communities. Binding these words "as a sign" on hands and heads and writing them on doorposts were ways for the Hebrews to proclaim identity, much in the way present-day bumper-sticker slogans say something about who we are and what we love. In addition, the community is to teach the commandment to the children and talk about it at the dinner table, at work, and on the road. To Israel, daily family prayer and the weekly Sabbath were the centers of family life. The purpose of the Sabbath celebration was both to bind Israel together as a people and to remind them of what God had done for them.

In addition to regular ceremonies in the home, in which the father was the primary teacher, teaching and learning continued in informal settings. Patrick Miller comments:

The picture is that of a family continually in lively conversation about the meaning of their experience with God and God's expectations of them. Parental teaching of the children by conversation about "the words," study of God's instruction, and reflection on it is to go on in the family and the community. Whether at or away from home, "these words" are to be uppermost in mind and heart; parents should teach their children in such a way that their last thoughts before falling asleep and their first words upon getting up are about the Lord's command. The text is clear that "these words" are not simply to be recited or repeated. They are to be talked about—that is, discussed, studied, and learned.[6]

For the Hebrews, then, religious teaching began in the home with a form of traditioning that was indeed the communication of ways of knowing, ways of being, and ways of doing. In observation of their parents and imitation of them, through participation in family rituals, and in constant conversation, the "Word" came alive for the children. They learned what God had done and was continuing to do for them. They learned how they should live. This traditioning process was so important that Moses' final words in Deuteronomy are "Take to heart all the words . . . give them as a command to your children" (32:46–47).

But in the Old Testament, the responsibility to teach was not limited to parents. As faithful Israelites, the entire adult community had the responsibility for teaching the faith to which they were committed, telling the story of what God had done for them in the past, and laying out what God expected of them in response. Through this kind of traditioning, a way of life was transmitted from generation to generation. It was done through mentoring and modeling and in structured teaching situations that gave directions and guidance about what the Torah meant for daily living. Jeremiah acknowledges this community responsibility for traditioning when he describes the day of the "new covenant" when such teaching of one another will no longer be necessary, "for they shall all know me" (Jer. 31:34).

Traditioning also took place as the community gathered for worship. The liturgy itself became a focal point in the teaching process, as the people sang psalms that expressed the shared history of the believing and worshiping community. Among the psalms that portray the story of Israel are Psalms 78, 105, 106, 135, and 136. They tell of God's dealings with Israel from the very beginning of its history to the entrance into the Promised Land and—in the case of Psalm 78—as far as the raising up of David as "the anointed one." Psalm 78 states its traditioning purpose:

> We will tell to the coming generation
> the glorious deeds of the LORD, and his might,
> and the wonders that he has done.
>
> (Ps. 78:4b)

The Importance of Traditioning

When worship is seen as a way of affirming what it means to be God's people and of handing on the inherited faith story, it has power to strengthen the community's identity and shape its values and behavior.

TEACHING THROUGH FEASTING

The great religious feasts of the Old Testament were also occasions for traditioning. They provided opportunities for binding Israel as a community through shared celebrations and rituals and for reminding Israel of its unique heritage. The vivid and unforgettable ceremonies that marked these feasts provided graphic visual teaching and learning moments for both children and adults.

For example, the Passover ceremony, a part of the Feast of Unleavened Bread, was meant to be a form of experiential learning. Before the Passover, parents and children would diligently search the whole house in order to remove all unleavened bread. This action occasioned questions from the children, and the father would explain to them the meaning of the action. The Passover ritual itself directs children to ask their fathers during the ceremony, "What does this action mean?" (see Exod. 12:26–27). The father then explains the significance of the Passover by replying, "This is the Passover sacrifice of the Lord."

During the Feast of Booths, or Sukkot, when families came to Jerusalem for the fall harvest festival, each household built a shelter from leafy branches and lived outdoors during the seven days of the feast, to recall that they were a pilgrim people who had lived in tents in the wilderness. A child could hardly forget when learning through such active involvement and participation. Even today this continues to be true. A Jewish friend remembers, "I will never forget the excitement we had during the Feast of Booths. My father always built a shelter in the yard, and we slept outdoors! We children always looked forward to it, even though we didn't get much sleep because of the twigs and leaves that kept falling down from the roof of the shelter! Sukkot was a special time of remembering God's deliverance."

The central focus of the feasts was the telling of the Exodus story, so that Israel would not forget what God had done in liberating and sustaining them as a people. The pilgrim feasts in Jerusalem were such a vital part of this remembering that when the Temple was destroyed in 70 A.D. and the cohesive rituals of sacrifices and pilgrim festivals could no longer be practiced, it became more difficult for the Jewish people to sustain and pass on their identity to subsequent generations. It was to counteract this loss that Rabbi Johannon ben Zakkai developed a seminary at Jamnia, to strengthen the authority of the Pharisaic rabbis as keepers of the tradition.

TRADITIONING BY THE PROPHETS AND THE WISDOM TEACHERS

The teachings of the prophets continued the practice of traditioning. Walter Brueggemann suggests that one method the prophets used to relieve the despair of the people was to offer symbols—not new symbols but ones that came from the deepest memories of the community. "The symbols of hope cannot be general and universal but must be those that have been known concretely in this particular history."[7] Through the use of symbols that rearticulated the old, old stories, Israel's faith was renewed in times of desperation, such as the exile.

The wisdom teachers in Israel performed two functions. For one thing, they provided formal education for wealthy youth in court schools, training them to be future rulers and leaders. But the wisdom teachers also took seriously the task of traditioning youth not destined to be rulers in the values of the community. They identified acceptable conduct and warned about the dangers of violating the community's standards and earning its disapproval. Sometimes this education took the form of didactic instruction, sometimes the form of proverbs or numerical sayings. The book of Proverbs provides many examples of this kind of teaching.

TRADITIONING IN NEW TESTAMENT TIMES

In the postexilic period, those most responsible for traditioning were the scribes who wrote down the Law and Prophets. The Pharisees were the most influential group among these scribes.They were looked up to as guardians of the tradition, the official interpreters of the Torah, and living models to follow. They included in their canon of scriptures not only the five books of Moses but the Prophets and the Writings, which articulated their hopes for the coming of the messiah. They believed that the law given to Moses consisted of both the written Law (the Torah) and the oral law (unwritten religious tradition). The oral tradition could always be enlarged, which meant that it was flexible and adjustable. By the first century A.D., a canon of Hebrew scriptures existed, although this was not formally fixed until the Synod of Jamnia met circa 100 and reviewed the collection of Jewish sacred writings.

Because of the Pharisees' belief in the vital importance of both oral instruction and imitating the living teacher, they stressed apprenticeship rather than theoretical learning. Disciples of Pharisaic rabbis spent a great deal of time with their teachers, following them from village to village, observing their teaching as well as their actions. They learned in community with others who were expected to ask questions and debate the meaning of texts with enthusiasm and eagerness. One of the Jewish writings contains this humorous and graphic picture of learners:

> There are four types of pupils of the wise men: a sponge, a funnel, a strainer, and a sieve. A sponge which absorbs everything; a funnel which lets in at one end and out of the other; a strainer which lets the wine pass and retains the sediment; a sieve which lets out the bran dust and retains the fine flour. (*Pirqe, Abot,* 6:8)

Anyone who has tried to teach will recognize that this description is just as true of learners today.

JESUS AS TRADITIONER

What was Jesus' understanding of traditioning? Like the Pharisees, he held the Torah in high regard; but he rejected the oral tradition of interpretation, which the Pharisees held as equally authoritative with the Torah. Jesus wanted to return to the essence of the covenant and to provide a new basis for interpreting the Law. He considered the Torah to be not a system of regulations but a way of life, lived in obedience to God and with compassion toward others.

His methods of traditioning, however, were much like those used by the Pharisees. He gathered around him a group of learners, whom he regularly taught: correcting their misunderstandings about the Torah, turning upside down their most cherished notions about righteousness and the kingdom of heaven. The crowds called him Rabbi, an honorary title given to those whose gift for teaching and knowledge of the Law were recognized.

No one in scripture was more interested in teaching than Jesus. He is referred to as a teacher, or didáskálos forty-eight times in the Gospels. He did not use the rabbinic style of teaching, which depended mainly on exact repetition of the teacher's words, but spoke in a spontaneous style that addressed immediate situations. He knew the Hebrew scriptures and often referred to them or quoted them in an effort to help his disciples and followers discover their true meaning.

But most important, Jesus taught not only by words but by the example of his life. His favorite command was "Follow me," or "Come after me." He was a practical teacher who showed people concrete ways to live out the Torah. Even his miracles were intended to teach about God's presence and power.

Jesus gave us a model of what it means to be a guardian of the tradition: to know the scripture, to address immediate situations with its wisdom, to model its truth by living it, to pass on to others what it means to belong to the family of God.

PAUL AND THE EARLY CHURCH

Paul also understood clearly the importance of traditioning. He constantly spoke of himself as a teacher and exhorted Christians in the early church to take the role of teacher seriously. In one of his letters to the Corinthians, he ranks teachers only after apostles and prophets in importance (1 Cor. 12:28), and in Ephesians they are mentioned among those who have received gifts from the risen Christ "to equip the saints for the work of ministry, for building up the body of Christ" (Eph. 4:12). In Romans he calls teaching a gift of grace (Rom. 12:7).

In Paul's letters to Timothy, he makes twenty-nine references to teaching or instruction, stressing the urgency for sound teaching based on scripture, teaching whose aim is "love that comes from a pure heart, a good conscience, and sincere faith" (1 Tim. 1:5). He reminds Timothy to "hold to the standard of sound teaching that you have heard from me, in the faith and love that are in Christ Jesus. Guard the good treasure entrusted to you, with the help of the Holy Spirit living in us" (2 Tim. 1:13–14). No clearer statement could be made about the way traditioning binds people together in faith and reminds them who they are.

One of the most striking aspects of Paul's traditioning method is its emphasis on imitation. Paul believed strongly that he was a link between the churches he had founded and Jesus himself. Because of this, he presents himself as an example of Christian tradition that is to be handed on to others, saying, "You yourselves know how you ought to imitate us" (2 Thess. 3:7–9). He reminds Timothy how Timothy has observed his teaching, his conduct, his aim in life, his faith, his patience, his love, his steadfastness, and also his persecutions and suffering, and then Paul urges him to continue in what he has learned (2 Tim. 3:10, 14). Paul is always careful to add that his followers are to imitate him because he is an imitator of Christ, pointing back to the gospel on which he has based his life.

Although Paul emphasizes that others should learn from his example, it is clear that the foundation of the tradition he wants to pass on is made up of "the sacred writings that are able to instruct you for salvation through faith in Christ Jesus" (2 Tim. 3:15). The writings to which Paul refers are the Torah, Psalms, and Prophets, since the New Testament writings that had been written were not yet canonized. Paul's attitude toward his Jewish heritage is one of profound gratitude, but he saw that heritage "as a still transmuting, evolving tradition preeminently becoming fulfilled in the preaching of the incarnate and risen Lord." By viewing Christianity as a fulfillment of Jewish tradition, not a departure from it, he put a high value on understanding and teaching that tradition.[7]

The Importance of Traditioning

The early church saw itself as a missionary church and put great emphasis on the need for training to make an effective witness to the gospel in the world. Paul wanted his fellow Christians to be teachers "rightly explaining the word of truth" (2 Tim. 2:15). It was especially important, in an environment hostile to their message, that Christians be clear about their identity and beliefs, so teaching was an important part of the baptismal experience. A period of instruction and reflection was considered necessary for both Jewish and Gentile converts, to ensure that they understood their new faith clearly and could bear convincing witness to it. Converts needed skilled teachers to lead them through the learning process, teachers well versed not only in the tradition of the Hebrew scriptures but in the stories of Jesus' life, teachings, and ministry. It is impossible to understand the story of Jesus without understanding the Old Testament tradition that stands behind him, so the Old Testament stories and teachings were important to early Christians, both in their own right and in order to foster understanding of what it meant that Jesus came to "fulfill the law."

As time went on, teachers became increasingly important. They were to take seriously the responsibility of passing on to the church a clear understanding of Jesus' teachings, so that false teachers ("savage wolves," according to Paul; see Acts 20:28–31), who were distorting the true gospel message, might be recognized. Paul knew that people have a tendency to "accumulate for themselves teachers to suit their own desires, and will turn away from listening to the truth and wander away to myths" (2 Tim. 4:3–4). For this reason, Paul urged Timothy to "convince, rebuke, and encourage, with the utmost patience in teaching" (2 Tim. 4:2). Good, careful traditioning helps guard against misunderstandings and error.

TRADITIONING AND THE CHURCH TODAY

Traditioning, the telling and retelling of our family faith stories, is crucial to the life of the church. It binds us together and reminds us who we are. The Bible is not only the foundation piece in our traditioning; it models in itself the importance of "telling the old, old story."

Both the Old and New Testaments reveal that the people of God depended on teachers who could clearly and intelligently articulate the family story, so that generation after generation could join in that shared meaning. If the church is to survive in today's world, then it must take seriously the urgent task of training and equipping the same kind of "traditioners," who will bind the people of God and remind them who they are.

2.

Called to Teach

I remember clearly the moment I felt a "call." I was sixteen and was attending a large youth conference on the world mission of the church. At the closing worship service cards were distributed, and we were asked to sign one if we felt "called to full-time Christian service." As I wrote my name on that small orange card, I felt an upsurge of altruism, excitement, humility, commitment, and faith that marked the moment as a definitive one in my life. I believed firmly that God called me into service in the church. I had no way of knowing, at that moment, what form such service would take, but of one thing I was sure: it was not a call to the ministry of Word and sacrament, since the Presbyterian Church in the United States did not ordain women in 1946.

Since that time I have filled many roles in the church: Sunday school teacher, elder, secretary, Christian educator, overseas missionary, campus minister, and, finally, minister of Word and sacrament. In each of these roles, I felt distinctly that I was answering the call I had experienced at age sixteen. When I was finally ordained a minister in 1984, I felt that in some sense it was a retroactive ordination, imparting the sign and seal of the church's blessing on that call which had begun forty-eight years before.

Was that call an illusion? The emotional response of an idealistic teenager? Does a call pertain only to professional clergy? I do not believe any of these is true.

One of the most consistent ironies in Protestant church life is the way in which our voices loudly affirm our belief in "the priesthood of believers" yet our behavior denies a commitment to it. For instance, most lay people, if asked, "Are you called to ministry?" would respond, "Oh, no! I'm just a layperson." In their eyes, and in the not-too-subtle rhetoric of the church, *ministry* is a professional term, belonging to only one kind of vocation.

In the New Testament, the Greek word for clergy (klêros) is used to express the inheritance and the ordination (or being chosen by lot) of all the laity (see Col. 1:12; Eph. 1:11; Gal. 3:29). So in the biblical sense, everyone is a clergyperson. It took three centuries for the church to use the word *layperson* to mean "nonprofessional," distinguishing lay people from *clergy*, who had received specialized training for ministry. From that time on, the misunderstanding emerged that clergy ministered and the laity received the ministry of the clergy.[1]

As a result of this misunderstanding, the church sees the necessity of scrupulously preparing clergy for ministry but neglects the preparation of its lay people. Most denominations require seminary preparation for pastors before they can be ordained and also expect pastors to pursue continuing education after ordination. Denominational judicatories and congregational governing bodies examine, test, approve, and confirm clergy calls. These calls are recognized and celebrated in special ordination ceremonies.

However, the church has no similar expectation or provision of preparation for lay people who feel called to ministry, and most churches greet their calls with very little liturgical celebration. Our current policies for calling lay leaders into the church's ministries are careless and haphazard, seeming almost designed to discourage persons with the most potential and to cater to the half-hearted and lackadaisical. If it were not for the saving influence of the Holy Spirit, which moves people to want to serve God with their talents, the church would be in sad shape indeed.

Another result of the neglect of lay ministry is the denigration of the role of the nonordained professional church educator. I have experienced the pain of having my ministry as a lay educator viewed as much less significant than that of the pastor simply because the pastor was ordained. And if professional educators receive substandard treatment, even more so do other lay people who feel God's call to ministry. Jim Stockard, an active layperson in Cambridge, Massachusetts, believes that his work as a consultant for low-cost housing development *is* ministry and issues a blunt challenge: "Until clergy can enthusiastically relinquish their 'more equal' status among God's people, I see little possibility for calling forth the ministries of the whole people of God."[2]

The reality is twofold: (1) all Christians are called into ministry by virtue of their baptisms, and (2) the work of the kingdom is everyone's task. To deny this reality is to make a theological error of great significance. To deny it trivializes the meaning of the body of Christ and jeopardizes the vitality of its life. To deny it leaves ministry in the hands of a few and encourages the "let Rev. George (or Georgina) do it" attitude that haunts our churches. To deny it is to deny the biblical vision of the people of God.

COVENANT AND CALL

The Old Testament makes clear that God's call extended to the entire community of the chosen people. Being called was a part of the covenant relationship. To be an Israelite meant to be subject to that call. The covenant was more than just a contract, an exchange of goods or services; God's people were more than just "hired hands," who would serve God in return for God's protection and favor. God called, and the people responded to that call not out of duty, but out of a sense of unity and belonging. They were called to be God's people.

The New Testament continues this understanding of a general call to all of God's people. The Greek word for church, *ekklēsia*, literally means those who are "called out" to be the body of Christ, those who are a part of the new covenant. The letter to the Hebrews is addressed to "holy partners in a heavenly calling" (Heb. 3:1). Paul was particularly sensitive to the idea of being called and urged the Ephesians to "lead a life worthy of the calling to which you have been called" (Eph. 4:1). He reminded Timothy how God "called us with a holy calling, not according to our works but according to his own purpose and grace" (2 Tim. 1:9). And who can forget Paul's stirring cry: "I press on toward the goal for the prize of the heavenly call of God in Christ Jesus" (Phil. 3:14)?

In both the Old and New Testaments, it is evident that within that general call to the whole covenant community, some were called to specific tasks, among them Abraham, Moses, Joshua, Deborah, David, Isaiah, Paul, Barnabas, Luke, Dorcas, and Timothy. Paul speaks of these special tasks when he says, "Some would be apostles, some prophets, some evangelists, some pastors and teachers," adding that all of these are "to equip the saints for the work of ministry, for building up the body of Christ" (Eph. 4:11–12). George Peck, professor of Christian Theology and International Mission at Andover Newton Seminary, clarifies the distinction between a general call to God's people and specific calls to the tasks of ministry by saying, "The call to ministry is a *specific* thing that comes in the midst of the general call to discipleship and is linked to a number of distinct elements. It is issued to all believers, in different ways, and for different purposes."[3]

How does one go about determining one's specific call to ministry? Peck suggests using the following criteria for all believers, not just pastors: a sense of being led by the Holy Spirit; the presence of certain gifts and of opportunities for their use; being prepared for the use of those gifts; having one's call recognized by others; being commissioned, appointed, supported, and held accountable by the church.[4]

Specific calls are a part of our exploration of what it means to be in covenant relationship with God. As we grow in awareness of the special gifts we have been given, we want to use these gifts as an extension of Jesus' ministry. We are called to ministry and empowered for it through our baptism, but our faith task is to respond to the question, "Where is Christ inviting me to serve?"

DISCERNING OUR GIFTS

If we acknowledge that the word *call* has been misused and is not limited to those whom God has chosen to serve as "pastors," then the church has some serious retooling to do. We must find ways to discern the gifts of all members of the body of Christ, to invite them to recognize calls to particular tasks within that body, and to provide appropriate preparation for those who feel called to specific tasks.

There are many ways to discern gifts. Perhaps the most frequently used (and abused) approach is that of the "time and talent inventory." This often appears as a questionnaire on which church members can indicate the areas in which they are willing to serve. They can check items such as "Teach a class of children," "Be an adult leader of youth," and "Sing in the choir." Although some useful information may be gathered this way (for instance, it helps in unearthing much-needed piano players), the process has several flaws.

First, many people think that filling out the questionnaire means committing to a task, and they are not ready for a specific commitment. Second, in contrast to the first group, some may feel disappointed because they have indicated a willingness to serve in a specific area but no call ever comes. And third, the return on questionnaires is extremely small and rarely an accurate assessment of talents. Few people bother to reply, and even worse, those who do seldom allow the real person to surface. They tend to reduce the understanding of a call to an artificial matchup of talents and tasks, without much thought or prayer.

An Alban Institute publication, *The Equipping Pastor*, offers a better approach: distributing cards on which church members are asked to write their names and the answer to the simple question "If time, talent, and training were not obstacles, what would you really like to do for God in the church or world?"[5]. A variation on this was described by one pastor who asked every communicant in his church to take stock of his or her life and write him a letter. His instructions were: "Look at the stewardship of your life—your natural abilities and your opportunities—and tell me in letter form about yourself. What obedience is the Lord calling you to? What thing is God commanding? What are your dreams for your life, for this body, and for the interplay between the two?"[6]

Questions such as these allow for the movement of the Holy Spirit and a deeper consideration of what it means to be called by God to specific tasks. They can be catalysts for an exploration of one's gifts, aspirations, and duties. Presbyterian minister and author Frederick Buechner has provided a classic definition of call as the place where "your deep gladness and the world's deep hunger meet."[7] When issues of obedience, ability, dreams, and opportunities are faced with openness and yielding, the result can be the beginning of a serious commitment to ministry.

THE CALL TO TEACH

Among the specific calls that come to the priesthood of believers, says Paul, is that of teacher: the one who has the ministry of traditioning, of passing on the stories, teachings, and lore that make the community unique. Teaching requires special gifts: knowledge, aptitude, patience, enthusiasm, eagerness to learn and grow. How does the church go about finding persons with such gifts and extending to them a call to teach?

The traditional approach is to turn the job over to a committee on personnel or leadership training. This committee reviews the teaching positions that need to be filled and the gifts of congregational members. When the committee discovers a match between a job's requirements and a person's gifts, the committee asks that person to consider prayerfully a call to teach.

This approach has several weaknesses. First, it is a typical cart-before-the-horse plan. Persons are invited to consider a call to a teaching task before they have been adequately prepared for it. Second, this approach is predicated on the assumption that determining the gifts of congregational members and matching them to a job is a simple matter. The reality is that such matches are as tricky as a computer dating service. Although this is the most commonly used approach, it often results in decisions made on the skimpiest of perceptions and assumptions.

CREATING A PROGRAM

The best, most theologically sound approach to identifying and recruiting leaders, especially those who will serve as teachers, is one that will equip the saints for the work of ministry before asking them to consider a call to a specific task.

This approach involves a careful, thoughtful procedure of recruitment that allows room for the Holy Spirit's guidance and direction, is not coercive or threatening to participants, and provides concrete preparation in the basics of the Christian faith and the principles of good teaching and learning. It also provides opportunities for new member education, officer training, and in-service teacher training. Each segment could be open to any adult as an elective study course.

This procedure takes time and effort. It is not accomplished overnight. But I have seen the remarkable excitement and energy that it generates and have witnessed its effect in the lives of those who have participated in it. Not all who participated became teachers immediately, but all who took part gained a clearer understanding of their faith and were better equipped for future ministries.

The process consists of several stages: planning, recruiting, implementing, evaluating. All are essential. I recommend that planning and recruiting begin in January for training sessions to be held from September to May. Then June, July, and August are months for apprenticeship, and by the second fall, those who have completed the program may embark on the teaching ministries to which they have been called.

The following is a suggested timetable for an effective program of leadership training.

January:
Obtaining Approval and Ownership

How does it all begin? Although the initial enthusiasm for an intensive training program such as this one may come from a key leader (pastor, educator, Christian education committee chairperson), the program needs wider ownership if it is to succeed. It is important, therefore, that the key leader seek to involve the congregation's governing body from the beginning of the process. In many denominations, the approval of that body is required before any actual steps are taken. The key leader should make a clear explanation of the program to the governing body and detail exactly what is involved in carrying the program out.

The governing body then does the following:

1. Approves a special nine-month leadership training class. This class will include three segments: basic biblical overview, basic Christian beliefs, and basic principles of good teaching. (If possible, this class should be offered twice one week: Sunday morning during the Sunday school hour and on one weeknight. In this way, sessions missed on Sunday can be made up during the week. Teachers currently serving on Sundays would also be able to take the classes on weeknights.)

2. Appoints a special task force to carry out the details of

planning and recruiting for the leadership training class. This task force should consist of members of the Christian education committee, the pastor, the church educator, and others who know the congregation well and have an enthusiasm for the ministry of education.

February:
The Task Force Begins Work

It is wise for the task force to begin its work in an atmosphere of prayer and with a clear understanding of the importance of preparation for the task of traditioning the faith. Perhaps the key leader could summarize some of the principal ideas in the first two chapters of this book.

The first responsibility of the task force is to secure competent teachers for the three segments of the leadership training class. It is not necessary for the same person to teach all three segments. Possible teachers include the church staff, retired pastors and church educators in the area, college professors and public school teachers, judicatory staff, and members of the congregation who have above-average knowledge of the Bible and Christian doctrine and good teaching skills. If the task force invites guest teachers, it should offer them a modest honorarium.

The second responsibility of the task force is to select the persons who will receive special invitations to participate in the class. Task force members review the church roll and identify those considered to have leadership potential. The list must be as comprehensive as possible. Decisions should not be made on the basis of whether or not the task force members think someone would be willing to participate. Names are eliminated only when there is a strong negative feeling about the individual on the part of any member of the task force.

When the task force has compiled its list of names, it submits the list to the church's governing body for approval. These important steps not only stress the serious nature of the invitation to prospective participants but recognize the responsibility of the governing body for those engaged in the teaching ministry of the church.

March:
Inviting Participants

The task force requests that the pastor send a letter of invitation to those names approved by the governing body. This letter should make it clear that the recipient has been selected because of leadership potential, has been endorsed by the governing body, and has been invited to participate in a leadership training class but is under no obligation to teach at the end of the course. Such a letter might look something like this:

Dear_____,

You have been identified by the governing body of our church (Session, Council, etc.) as a person with leadership potential. The Session invites you to participate in a special leadership class to help you develop that potential. This leadership program begins in the fall and lasts for nine months. It includes intensive training on three topics: Bible study, Christian beliefs, and principles of good teaching.

Toward the end of the class, you may be asked to consider a call to serve in one of the church's educational programs. If you accept this call, you will have an opportunity to serve as an "apprentice" in the summer months, under skilled leaders, before assuming the responsibility yourself.

Taking the leadership class does not obligate you in any way. It will, however, give you the kind of background preparation we believe leaders need *before* they accept a call to a task. We ask that you consider this invitation prayerfully for several days. If you decide that you would like to be a part of this exciting new opportunity, please contact (the chair of the task force) by this date:_____.

Sincerely,
Your Pastor

April:
Making Arrangements

As recipients of the letter of invitation begin to respond to it, the task force takes care of housekeeping details, such as determining where the class shall be held; deciding how to advertise the courses, if they are to be opened up as adult electives; securing videos and learners' books; making sure that the resources and materials the teachers need are available; and developing a list of substitute teachers to call on.

September–May:
Training, Evaluation, and Presenting the Call

The class begins! Although not all members of the task force may be able to take the class, because of other responsibilities they may have, it is advisable to have representatives of the task force in each segment for an effective final evaluation.

Toward the end of the second segment of the leadership class, the task force meets to survey the church's leadership needs for the next year and to select prayerfully certain class participants whom it will invite to consider calls to fill these specific needs. Selections are made on the basis of the qualifications, aptitudes, and interests of the participants.

The task force prepares a one-page job description of each call and a written contract defining the length of the term of service, which will be signed by the chair of the task force, the pastor, and the person who accepts the call. An example of this contract is found on page 115 of chapter 6.

The task force must present calls to specific tasks through personal visits. This is a very important step in the process. Members of the task force should schedule individual appointments with the selected class participants in order to describe clearly the task to be considered, to affirm the participants' gifts that qualify them for this particular ministry, and to answer their questions. It is helpful if the visits can be made in teams of two.

When you approach the people you are calling, remind them that they are being given an opportunity to make a faith commitment, a covenant response to God's call. They are not being asked just to "fill a slot." But under no circumstances should anyone pressure a candidate to accept. Rather, ask the selected participant to take time to consider prayerfully the questions "Do my gifts suit me for this task?" and "Is this where Christ wants me to serve?"

Each interview should provide concrete information about the specific call. The task force team provides the person with the one-page job description and a copy of the contract to sign if he or she wishes to make a commitment.

June–August:
Preparing through Apprenticeship

If you have a summer program, the task force submits the names of class members who have expressed a willingness to teach to the church school superintendent or church educator, requesting that the candidates be given a chance to observe or substitute teach during the summer.

September:
Commissioning and Recognizing Those Called

The task force, working with the church staff, plans for the commissioning of new teachers. It is extremely important that those who are answering calls to specific ministries be commissioned for their tasks in a special service of recognition and encouragement, much like an ordination ceremony. In this way, the whole congregation affirms the call of these individuals and the sacredness of the commitment they are undertaking.

In his commentary on Deuteronomy, Patrick D. Miller sees the commissioning of Joshua (Deut. 31:7–8, 14–15, and 23) as reflecting a formal procedure of installation or commission that is also found in other places in the Old Testament. Miller says this proceeding could serve as "a model for occasions of installation and commissioning of new leaders." It contains the following elements:

1. Words of encouragement: "Be strong and bold" (31:7)
2. Description or assignment of the task
3. Divine reassurance: "The Lord will be with you" (31:8)

Miller sees in this form of commissioning the important elements "for all occasions when persons are given responsibility over the community of faith." The starting point is courage and confidence; then comes reiteration that the call is not to a position but to a task; and finally, "neither arrogant pride nor despairing anxiety is appropriate because the Lord is there and will not fail."[8]

By taking these three elements as a framework, it is possible to design a commissioning service that affirms a person's call and reminds the individual of the help that is available to him or her through the Lord's presence. Suggestions for such a service are found in chapter 6.

Although the work of the task force officially comes to an end with this service, its members can continue to provide valuable support and encouragement to new teachers throughout the year with words of appreciation and gratitude for their ministry.

This timetable is flexible and must be adapted to the individual church's situation. The work of the task force is crucial and will ensure effective coordination of all the components of the program. Staff assistance is very helpful, but staff should not have to be responsible for all the details.

With this schedule firmly in mind, it is time to turn our attention to the next three chapters, which outline what will be taught in the three segments of the course.

3.

Basic Biblical Background

If we believe that the Bible is inspired, that it reveals God to us, and that through it God continues to speak to the church, then it becomes of the utmost importance that our traditioning be, first and foremost, in the scriptures. This is a serious responsibility. In the limited time we have for teaching the faith, we must make the best possible use of the primary source, God's Word itself. If we are to re-present our faith accurately and honestly, then it is essential that those to whom we entrust the task of traditioning have a solid foundation in biblical knowledge. A three-month course cannot accomplish miracles, but it can provide an understanding of scripture as the unfolding of God's purposeful acts in history and of how the Bible's diverse parts are connected. The best possible result would be that this course proves an appetite whetter for further study.

This book is designed to implement just three months of training in Bible, but religious educator Robin Maas, author of *The Church Bible Study Handbook*, issues a wider challenge to pastors:

> Pastors should be concerned that the people the community relies on to transmit the faith through the teaching of scripture be nurtured *by scripture* on a regular basis. Who sees to it that these faithful ones who are called on week after week to give of themselves have opportunities to be spiritually challenged *at their own level of development?* It is unrealistic to expect that the "teacher's guide" supplied by the curriculum writers will do the trick; its function is simply to help the teacher in presenting the material clearly and effectively. My own experience has taught me that if volunteer religious educators are given an opportunity to explore the biblical material together as a group of adults committed to a common mission, enthusiasm for teaching the Bible to others will be sustained.[1]

Is it too much to ask that pastors share the rich training in Bible they have received with those whom the church has called to the task of traditioning the faith? It is my hope that this kind of ongoing interaction between teachers and pastors will be one of the fruits of the leadership development class.

Basic Biblical Background

INTERPRETING THE BIBLE

Any Bible survey course must deal with the issue of biblical interpretation. Those who feel called to pass on the tradition of the Christian faith need to have some understanding of how to read and interpret scripture. Scholars have contributed to this understanding by introducing us to the literary and historical contexts of the Bible's various books. Unfortunately, we have done little to pass on these helpful insights through our Christian education programs. As a result, most laypersons do not have an adequate foundation on which to base their interpretation of scripture. The result is "proof-texting"— taking passages out of context to prove a point.

Some years ago, I heard a story about a turn-of-the-century preacher that illustrates how ludicrous the practice of proof-texting can become. When women began to pile their long hair on their heads in elaborate knots, the preacher was convinced that such vanity was surely "of the devil." He searched through scripture to find an appropriate text for a sermon against the practice. On Sunday morning, he announced, "My text is from Matthew 24:17: 'Top knot come down!'" He had found what he wanted by editing out the first part of the verse: "Let him which is on the housetop not come down" (KJV).

As important as understanding the context of the biblical books is, however, the Bible is more than just a collection of literary and historical documents. The story of the Bible is the story of God's creation, subsequent human failure, God's redemptive activity, and human response. It is a story told in many ways and in different times. We read it and study it not just because it provides interesting data on times past but because of its relevance for our lives. We read it because it is where, as John Calvin said, "God is truly and vividly described to us."[2] It is a *living* text that provides us with the guidance, comfort, and nourishment we need as we struggle to be God's covenant people.

HELPFUL RESOURCES

It is important that each student have a Bible survey textbook for this segment. If budget constraints do not permit the church to purchase the student texts, then the initial letter to prospective class members should indicate the cost of the text, so that participants understand that purchasing the text is a part of their commitment. I recommend Betty Sharp Harold's *A Bird's-Eye View of the Bible from Genesis to Revelation* (Louisville, Ky.: Bridge Resources, 1996) which is delightful, witty, and down-to-earth. It provides a brief summary of books of the Bible and concludes with a capsule summary of each book, noting information about the author(s), the book's contents, and its implications, as well as giving a "notable verse" from the book.

Other helpful Bible surveys that are in print at this writing are:

Bernhard Anderson, *The Unfolding Drama of the Bible*, 3d ed.
(Philadelphia: Fortress Press, 1988)

Duncan Ferguson, *Bible Basics: Mastering the Content of the Bible*
(Louisville, Ky.: Westminster John Knox Press, 1995)

Richard Hiers, *Reading the Bible Book by Book* (Philadelphia: Fortress
Press, 1988)

Arnold Rhodes, *The Mighty Acts of God* (Philadelphia: Westminster
Press, 1964)

You will also need a good Bible atlas, such as Harry T. Frank's *Atlas of Bible Lands*, rev. ed. (New York: Hammond, Inc., 1990).

Some very useful videotapes have been produced in the last few years. *Discovering the Bible* (Worcester, Penn.: Gateway Films, 1996) is a video series consisting of four half-hour programs of introductory information and stunning visual scenes of biblical settings. The first program, "Getting Acquainted," looks at how the Bible came to be written and organized. The second, "The Old Testament," shows how the Old Testament was developed and preserved, with interesting footage about the Dead Sea Scrolls. The third, "The New Testament," shows how the New Testament came to be written and how the canon was developed. The fourth, "Survival, Spread and Influence," describes how the Bible survived in spite of attempts to destroy it, how it was taught in the Middle Ages, and its influence on individual lives. This series is professionally produced and very viewer friendly. It comes with a *Leader's Guide* and reproducible student worksheets.

The *Bible Teacher Kit*, produced by Nashville's Abingdon Press (1994), is an excellent companion piece for this segment. The kit contains background articles on biblical literature, places, and periods of history; a glossary of biblical terms, with a pronunciation guide; a sixty-minute color videotape of Bible lands; a photocopiable time line and charts; and eight twenty-by-thirty-two-inch full-color maps of Bible lands. If your church cannot afford to purchase these resources, check with your denominational resource center about renting them.

Computer resources are proliferating rapidly. Commentaries, concordances, and Bible games are increasingly available. Check your denominational catalogs for information about these.

Finally, an excellent resource to use along with this course is Jim Davison's *The Year of the Bible* (Louisville, Ky.: Bridge Resources, 1996), a plan for involving the whole congregation in reading the entire Bible together in a year. It consists of a leader's guide and participants' books. It would be a wonderful supplement to this segment for the entire congregation to be involved in reading the Bible. Davison's monthly summary comments on Old and New Testament passages in the participant's book are clear and helpful.

SEGMENT 1: BASIC BIBLICAL BACKGROUND

Each segment of the leadership class contains thirteen sessions (three months of weekly sessions), each approximately one hour long. It should be made clear that students are expected to participate in all sessions, making up missed sessions at the alternate times when the class is offered (Sundays or weeknights). They are also expected to do assigned readings and homework before each session. Each student should bring to the session a Bible, survey text, notebook, and pencil and should take notes. Note taking helps learners to remember what they have heard and provides a helpful resource for future reference.

The temptation in most survey courses is to try to "cover the material" by lecturing, but participants gain much more if they are actively involved in the learning process. However, you may supplement the brief informational content with one of the recommended resource books, Bible dictionaries, commentaries, and encyclopedias. If you prefer the lecture method, make sure to reinforce the teaching with charts, diagrams, maps, and outlines that provide visual as well as auditory input. Use chalkboards, overhead projectors, and newsprint. Don't hesitate to borrow teaching pictures from the children's department; many of these are beautifully drawn, showing details of the tabernacle, Solomon's temple, and synagogues, and can be excellent teaching aides. Draw out from the participants what they have learned from their assigned reading by asking at the beginning of each session for new insights they have gained.

One more thing—begin each session with earnest, heartfelt prayer for open minds, eager hearts, and a willingness to be guided by the Holy Spirit. Only in this way can Bible study achieve its true goal: that learners will be drawn closer to the One they love and serve.

Outline of Sessions
1. Introduction to the Bible
2. The Prologue (Genesis 1—11)
3. The Patriarchs (Genesis 12—50)
4. The Exodus (Exodus–Deuteronomy)

5. The Promised Land (Joshua–Judges)
6. The Monarchy (1 Samuel–2 Chronicles)
7. The Writings (Job–Song of Solomon)
8. The Prophets (Isaiah–Malachi)
9. The Exile and Return (Ezra–Nehemiah)
10. The Gospels (Matthew–John)
11. The Early Church (Acts)
12. The Epistles (Romans–Jude)
13. Revelation

Session 1:
Introduction to the Bible

Preparation

Rent or purchase one of the videos mentioned in the resource section. Locate a videocassette recorder (VCR) for the classroom.

Make a copy of a blank map of Palestine for each learner.

Secure a large wall map of Palestine in biblical times, but do not display it until after learners have filled in their blank maps.

Opening (10 minutes)

Welcome class members and distribute outlines of the sessions, with home-work assignments.

Ask the class the following question, allowing time for thoughtful responses: "What does the Bible mean in your life?" Record their responses. Then ask, What caused you to feel that way? Again, allow time for responses.

After participants have finished their responses, comment that although the Bible is central to our Christian faith, most of us have only a hazy idea of how its various books are connected. Explain that over the next three months, this course will provide a rapid-fire overview of scripture in order to provide a clearer understanding of that connection. Remind the class that the course will be greatly enriching for them if they do the homework assignments and read the corresponding passages in their survey texts. Urge them to bring notebooks to class and to take notes.

Presentation (30 minutes)

An excellent way to begin the course is to use one of the videos mentioned in the resource section, above, to provide a background for biblical study. *Dis-*

Basic Biblical Background

covering the Bible introduces the books of the Bible, while the other videos concentrate on the geographical settings of biblical events.

If you are not able to obtain a video, make the following brief lecture about the physical features of the land of the Bible, using pictures, maps, and slides to illustrate your lecture:

The Holy Land is a territory of striking variations. It has five main regions: a narrow coastal plain, the central mountains that form its backbone, the rich and fertile Jordan Valley, the highlands east of the Jordan River (called the Golan Heights today), and the eastern desert. The predominant soils are sandy loams and clays. When the Israelites moved into Canaan, they were forced to occupy the mountain slopes because the Canaanites and Philistines were already settled in the fertile plains and valleys. The Israelites developed a method of retaining rainwater by carving cisterns into the rocky hills.

Palestine is a small land: about 125 miles from north to south and 56 miles east to west. Jerusalem is only twelve miles from the Dead Sea, and Nazareth is about sixty-five miles from Bethlehem. The weather is similar to that of southern California, with rains coming in the fall and spring (see Jer. 5:24). The average rainfall varies, from eight to ten inches in the Negev, which is the desert in the south, to about thirty inches in the north. The land is subject to drought—so much so that drought and famine are the most frequently mentioned calamities of biblical times.

Deuteronomy 8:7–8 lists the "seven blessings" the Israelites were to find in Canaan. They were symbols of the country's fertility: wheat, barley, vines, fig trees, pomegranates, olive trees, and honey. These foods form a good picture of the diet of the people as they settled into the land.

Learning more about the climate, geography, and agriculture of biblical lands enriches our understanding of the Bible.

Exploration (10 minutes)

Provide blank maps of the Holy Land and ask learners to try to locate well-known places, such as Jericho, Jerusalem, Bethlehem, Nazareth, the Sea of Galilee, the Jordan River, and the Dead Sea. Give them time to fill in the names as best they can on the blank maps. Then use a large wall map (or sketch a map on the chalkboard) to identify the correct locations of the places.

Response (5 minutes)

Ask learners to respond by completing the following phrase on slips of paper: "The Bible is. . . ." Suggest that they use a poetic image.

Conclusion (5 minutes)

Collect the slips of paper and read the responses aloud as a closing meditation.

Assignment for Next Time

Read the following passages from Genesis: 1–3:24.; 6:5–9:17; 11:1–9. Write down three words that describe God as revealed in these stories.

Session 2:
The Prologue (Genesis 1—11)

Preparation

Make a copy of the worksheet for each learner. (See Appendix, page 121.)

Opening (10 minutes)

Ask the learners to name the characteristics of God they discovered in the assigned chapters of Genesis. Record their responses on newsprint or chalkboard as they are giving them. If there are duplicate words, simply underline them.

Ask the class, What does this list say about the purpose of these chapters and how the Hebrew people felt about these stories? Allow time for discussion.

Presentation (10 minutes)

Make a brief presentation of the following ideas:

The first eleven chapters of Genesis are often referred to as "the prologue" to the scriptures. They consist of ancient stories that cannot be set into any historical frame and were not put into writing until around 500 to 300 B.C. They include the stories of Creation, the Fall, the Flood, and the Tower of Babel. These stories contain profound spiritual insights. They describe the wisdom, purpose, power, and goodness of God, the Creator of the universe. They explain the meaning and origin of life, the origin of evil, and what the relationship of human beings to God should be. They teach that God created human beings, whose lives find meaning in their obedience to God's will. When human beings disobey that will, their lives become tragic and broken. In these stories sin is real, and its effects are clearly seen in the accounts of the Fall, the Flood, and the Tower of Babel. Sin alienates human beings from God, from other people, and from their own true destinies.

These stories are sometimes referred to as *myths*, a term that may be upsetting because it seems to imply that they are untrue. In ancient times, the term *myth* referred to an account of how the gods acted in the world. Myths were ways to explain such mysteries as the origin of the universe. The stories in Genesis can be considered myths too, because they tell how the one true God acted to bring into existence the world and all that is and what God requires of human beings. Calling them myths in no way takes away from their truth. However, it was not the purpose of the biblical writers to give scientific and historical accounts of how creation took place. Religious matters and ideas, not historical specificity, were important to the Hebrews, especially in areas that humans could not have observed, such as the Creation.

Exploration (20 minutes)

Because these ancient stories were a part of Israel's oral tradition, many of them appear in several versions. An example of this can be seen in this exercise.

Divide the class into two groups. Give each person a copy of the worksheet (page 121). Assign one group Genesis 1:1–2:3 and the other Genesis 2:4–25. Remind the students they are to get their answers only from the passage they were assigned. Allow them to work ten minutes, then have the groups report their answers, one question at a time. Record their responses on a chalkboard or newsprint.

After all questions are answered, ask, What observations would you make after seeing these two lists of answers?[3] Point out that each of these accounts came from a different time and strand of tradition, and each had a different purpose.

Response (10 minutes)

Have learners create a cinquain (pronounced *sin*-kan) poem that expresses the characteristics of God revealed in these early stories. The first line contains the title (one word); the second line describes the title (two words); the third line contains action words (three words); the fourth line contains feeling words (four words); the fifth line is the conclusion (one word). Here is an example of a cinquain:

God
Life-giver, Sustainer
Working, blessing, grieving
Maker of good things
Creator

Conclusion (10 minutes)

Share aloud as many of the cinquains as time allows.

Assignment for Next Time

Where did each of the patriarchs (Abraham, Isaac, Jacob, Joseph) live? Use a Bible dictionary or review Genesis 12—50 to find the answer.

Ask for four volunteers willing to play the roles of these patriarchs in a "talk-show" interview in the next session. They should be prepared to answer the question "What was the most significant event in your life?"

Session 3:
The Patriarchs (Genesis 12—50)

Preparation

Secure maps showing the routes of the patriarchs. Maps are essential for this session. They can be wall maps, overhead projections, individual maps, or maps on video, but they must be used.

Arrange five chairs in the front of the class for the talk-show interviews. You, as interviewer, may sit behind a desk with the "guests" at one side.

Make copies of Hebrews 11:8–16 for the concluding unison reading.

Provide outline maps that include Egypt, Sinai, and Palestine.

Opening (5 minutes)

Introduce the patriarchs briefly as follows:

The journeys of Abraham, Isaac, Jacob, and Joseph are traced in the last part of Genesis. God makes a covenant with Abraham and his descendants: "I will be your God and you shall be my people." This promise was also given to Isaac and Jacob and marks the beginning of "the chosen people." The covenant promise included both "seed" and "land." The seed was Israel and the land was Canaan, although, ironically, none of the patriarchs possessed any of the land, except for the field Abraham bought for Sarah's burial place.

Then, using the maps, ask learners to identify the places where each of the patriarchs lived.

Basic Biblical Background

Presentation (30 minutes)

As talk-show host, introduce the four guests, one at a time: Abraham, Isaac, Jacob, and Joseph. Ask each guest this question: "What was the most significant event in your life?" Other questions may flow from this one. Guests will remain seated during one another's interviews.

Exploration (15 minutes)

Write the following locations and scripture references on newsprint or a chalkboard. Ask learners to read as many passages as time allows and note the following: the event, the name of the person appearing in the passage, and the significance of his or her encounter with God.[4]

> Haran (Gen. 12:4)
> Moriah (Gen. 22:2)
> Paddan-Aram (Mesopotamia) (Gen. 28:2)
> Bethel (Gen. 28:19)
> Peniel (Gen. 32:30)
> Egypt (Gen. 39:1)
> Canaan (Gen. 12:5)
> Nile River (Exod. 1:22)
> Midian (Exod. 2:16)

Response (10 minutes)

Ask as many learners as time permits to share something new they have learned about these persons' encounters with God.

Conclusion

Hand out copies of Hebrews 11:8–16 and ask the learners to read these verses in unison.

Assignment for Next Time

Read Exodus 19 and 20 and Deuteronomy 6.

Provide the class with outline maps of the world of the Old Testament. Ask participants to mark the route of the Israelites from Egypt to Canaan.

Session 4:
The Exodus (Exodus–Deuteronomy)

Preparation

Prepare a chart with the following brief descriptions. Use a different color for each book to make it more vivid.

THE EXODUS

Exodus: Tells of God's liberation of Israel from Egypt, under the leadership of Moses; details the covenant requirements in the wilderness; and reveals the expectation God has that Israel will obey the covenant obligations.

Leviticus: Provides instructions for the religious ceremonies and rituals that define the community.

Numbers: Recounts Israel's experiences in the wilderness, which included instances of both obedience and disobedience.

Deuteronomy: Recapitulates Israel's wanderings and the Ten Commandments and renews the call to obedience in the form of Moses' farewell address.

Opening (10 minutes)

Ask the class, After reading Exodus 19 and 20 and Deuteronomy 6, what do you think it means to be God's chosen people? List the class's answers on newsprint or a chalkboard.

Presentation (20 minutes)

Present the chart of Exodus, Numbers, Leviticus, and Deuteronomy that you have prepared. Comment on it briefly and allow time for questions. Emphasize that central themes in these chapters are the formation of Israel as a community and the importance of the Exodus experience as a primary symbol of God's protective care and liberating love.

Exploration (20 minutes)

Ask the participants, How many of the Exodus and wilderness events can you name? List the responses on newsprint. Ask the learners to number them chronologically, using Bibles or textbooks to help when necessary.

Ask the class, How did the people respond to God in these events?

Response (5 minutes)

Have the learners each choose one of the characters in these events and write an end to this sentence: "If I had been _____ I would have felt _____."

Conclusion (5 minutes)

Share as many sentence completions as time allows.

Assignment for Next Time

1. Read Joshua 1:1–9. List (1) God's promises and (2) God's expectations.
2. Review the book of Judges. List the names of the thirteen judges, noting how long each ruled.

Session 5:
The Promised Land (Joshua–Judges)

Opening (10 minutes)

Ask the class, When you have had to face an overwhelming responsibility that seemed almost too much for you, what got you through it? Allow time for responses, then ask, As you read the first chapter of Joshua, which verse or verses would have been a source of strength for you in that crisis?

Presentation (10 minutes)

Introduce the session with the following brief summary:

The occupation and gradual conquest of the Promised Land are described in Joshua and Judges. Israel began to add the worship of the agricultural gods of the Canaanites to its worship of God. This failure to keep the commandments inaugurated a cycle of backsliding, oppression, and deliverance that repeats itself over and over again throughout the book of Judges. The stories in Judges underscore the idea that God is present and active in history in ways we do not always understand.

Ask learners to list the judges (their homework assignment), indicating the ones who did not live up to God's expectations as described in Joshua 1.

Exploration (15 minutes)

Have a learner read aloud the story of Othniel in Judges 3:7–11. Ask, Where is the cycle of backsliding, oppression, and deliverance revealed in this story?

Response (20 minutes)

Divide the class into four groups and assign one of the following judges to each group. Each group should read the judge's story and develop a list of six words that describe the person.

> Deborah, Judges 4—5
> Gideon, Judges 6—8
> Jephthah, Judges 11
> Samson, Judges 13—16

Conclusion (5 minutes)

Call out the names of the four judges one at the time, and ask each group to share with the class its six descriptive words and, if they choose, the reasons they selected those words.

Read to the class Psalm 86:1–11 as a closing prayer.

Assignment for Next Time

1. What was God's covenant with David? See 2 Samuel 7:1–17.
2. What was the major cause of the split of the kingdom? See 1 Kings 12:1–4.

Session 6:
The Monarchy (1 Samuel–2 Chronicles)

Preparation

Prepare a chart that lists the rulers of the divided kingdom and the dates of their rule, with stars by the names of the few who were good rulers (Joash, Hezekiah, Josiah). (See Appendix, page 122.) Make copies for the class.

Opening (10 minutes)

Ask the class, What particular problems and temptations do rulers of nations in today's world face? Allow time for responses and write them on newsprint or chalkboard. Then ask, Which of these problems did the kings of Judah and Israel face?

Presentation (20 minutes)

Read Samuel's words of warning about kings in 1 Samuel 8:11–18.
Present a brief lecture similar to the following:
For 250 years, Israel had been a theocracy—a people ruled by God. Toward the end of Samuel's life, the people began to cry out for a warrior-king, such as other nations had. Reluctantly, Samuel anointed Saul, whose downfall was his flagrant disobedience of God's commands. David was established king first over his own tribe of Judah, then over the nation as a whole. He unified Israel and gave Israel security from its enemies through victories over surrounding tribes and city-states.

Have the learners discuss their responses to the homework assignment question about God's covenant with David. (The answer should be roughly that it established the promise of "a kingdom made sure forever before me," which would be realized in the coming Messiah.)

Next, ask the class to discuss the homework question about the cause for the split in the kingdom. (The answer should be roughly that Solomon's excesses, both sexual and political, prepared the way for the split in the nation during the reign of his son, Rehoboam.)

Explain that for the next two centuries, the nation suffered under a succession of despotic rulers who fulfilled Samuel's prophetic words. Israel's capture by Assyria and Judah's by Babylon were the beginning of the fifty-year period of the exile. The return to Jerusalem and the rebuilding of the city and the Temple under Ezra and Nehemiah mark the end of Old Testament history.

Exploration (15 minutes)

Distribute the chart listing the kings of the divided kingdom (page 122). Discuss the chart briefly, without spending too much time on individual kings. Make the point that Samuel's predictions were fulfilled in the behavior of these monarchs.

Response (10 minutes)

Ask each learner to write a position description for the kind of king God wanted and to share the descriptions with two other class members.

Conclusion (5 minutes)

The psalms called "the royal psalms" were written with kings in mind. One of these is Psalm 20, which is a prayer for the king. Ask the learners to read it silently and then to identify and discuss what is being prayed for.

Assignment for Next Time

Read Proverbs 3 and 4. Bring to class a "proverb" not found in the Bible that has meant something special to you. This could be a motto, an old saying, or a bumper-sticker slogan.

Session 7:
The Writings (Job–Song of Solomon)

Preparation

Bring to class plain white paper, construction paper, markers, white glue, pieces of paper cut into three-by-twenty-four-inch strips, magazines and newspapers, and scissors.

Opening (5 minutes)

Begin the class by asking learners to share the proverbs they brought to class. What do these suggest about the nature of proverbs and of wisdom literature in general?

Presentation (15 minutes)

Give the following presentation:

One of the most fascinating parts of the Old Testament is the section called "wisdom literature" in the English Bible and "the Writings" in the Hebrew Bible. In both cases, this section is actually an anthology. The books included are diverse in style and content but, when taken as a whole, form a valuable picture of the life and culture of Old Testament times. The Writings in the Hebrew Bible consists of the following books: Psalms, Song of Solomon, Lamentations, Job, Proverbs, Ecclesiastes, Ruth, Esther, 1 and 2 Chronicles, Ezra and Nehemiah, and Daniel.

In the English Bible, the wisdom literature anthology includes only Job, Psalms, Proverbs, Ecclesiastes, and the Song of Solomon. The diversity of these books is readily apparent from their subject matter. Job addresses the theme of human suffering and evil. Psalms is an anthology of religious poetry and songs. Proverbs is a collection of practical wisdom drawn from everyday life. Ecclesiastes explores the futility of human wisdom and effort. The Song of Solomon is an anthology of love poems.

Wisdom literature grew out of a philosophical approach that attempted to make sense out of life's big questions and little issues. It developed from two primary sources. The first was folk wisdom, which was wisdom "from below." It came from practical, everyday experience and had the twang of genuine honesty and hard-earned knowledge. The book of Proverbs is full of this kind of wisdom, for example, "All the days of the poor are hard, but a cheerful heart has a continual feast" (Prov. 15:15). Although many of these sayings seem more commonsensical than overtly religious, underlying them all is the agreement that "the fear of the LORD is the beginning of wisdom" (Prov. 9:10). The second form of wisdom lore was developed in the court schools where sages trained young men to become good leaders, emphasizing such traits as honesty, diligence, trustworthiness, and control of appetites. Wisdom literature is characterized by its use of proverbs, riddles, parables, and allegories.

The book of Job is the best example of the wisdom literature. It reflects the wisdom school's concern with the large philosophical issues of suffering, obedience, and faithfulness but questions the wisdom position (represented by Job's friends) that rewards and punishment are given to those who justly deserve them.

Many of the Psalms are classic wisdom literature, commending the way of righteousness as a way to reward (Pss. 1; 34; 37; 92). However, Psalm 73, like Job, dares to question this position, stating, "All in vain I have kept my heart clean" (73:13).

Ecclesiastes is a mixture of humor and irony, as its author, "the preacher," tries to discover how to live wisely and decides the best people can do is "to be happy and enjoy themselves as long as they live" (3:12). His approach has a very contemporary ring to it.

The Song of Solomon is a collection of the love poems of Israel. It was included in the wisdom collection because it underscored some very important "family values": mutuality and fidelity in love. In this it is similar to Proverbs 5:15–20, which urges faithfulness to "the wife of your youth, a lovely deer, a graceful doe."

Exploration (20 minutes)

Write the following instructions and questions on a chalkboard or newsprint. Ask the class to divide into groups of three to discuss the questions.

Proverbs: Browse through the book of Proverbs until you find a verse you would like your children or grandchildren to memorize. Share this proverb with the others.

Job: Was Job really a patient man? Find verses to support your opinion. Do Job and Proverbs disagree about God rewarding those who are good? If so, state why.

Ecclesiastes: Does Ecclesiastes have any religion? What can you find in this book that is redemptive?

Psalms: Do you agree with the philosophy suggested in Psalm 37:25: "I have been young, and now am old, yet I have not seen the righteous forsaken or their children begging bread"?

Hebrew wisdom: As you look at the whole sweep of biblical wisdom, does it give you a way of looking at life? Can you think of any modern writers who remind you of Hebrew sages?[5]

Response (15 minutes)

Have learners choose one of the following activities:

1. Write a short psalm based on your own experience of God's steadfast love. Mount your psalm on construction paper and tape it to the wall or chalkboard. (Provide the students with paper, construction paper, glue.)
2. Create a bumper-sticker slogan based on one of these proverbs: 11:28; 12:25; 13:24; 15:1; 16:17; 16:18; 17:1; 19:8; 22:6; 22:9. Tape the slogan to the wall. (Provide the learners with paper cut in three-by-twenty-four-inch strips and with markers)
3. Make a collage from newspaper and magazine pictures and words that illustrate the words from Ecclesiastes 1:2: " Vanity of vanities! All is vanity." Again, tape this to the wall or display it on a table.

Conclusion (5 minutes)

Ask class members to take time to enjoy their exhibit of literature and art as they leave the class. Leave the exhibit up until the next class.

Assignment for Next Time

What was the response of each of the following prophets to God's call: Isaiah (chap. 6), Jeremiah (chap. 1), Ezekiel (chaps. 1—2)?

Session 8:
The Prophets (Isaiah–Malachi)

Preparation

Make copies of articles in a Bible dictionary on these six prophets: Isaiah, Jeremiah, Hosea, Amos, Jonah, and Micah.

For the homework assignment, make copies of an outline map of the Middle East that shows Egypt and Palestine.

Opening (5 minutes)

Choose two participants to read Jeremiah's call in Jeremiah 1:4–10; have one read the words of Jeremiah and one the words of God. Ask your class, What can you learn about the role of a prophet from these verses?

Presentation (15 minutes)

Make the following presentation:

Written prophecy did not begin until the middle of the eighth century B.C., although Israel had already experienced the prophetic leadership of Samuel, Nathan, Elijah, Elisha, and others. The distinction between major and minor prophets has more to do with the length of the books than with their importance.

The role of the prophets was to speak for God to the people. They were "forth-tellers" more than "fore-tellers." Although they warned about future happenings in many cases, they also interpreted the past and gave guidance in the present. The primary emphasis of their predictions was on the establishment on earth of the reign of God, which often included predictions of the coming of the Messiah.

The greatest of all the prophets was Isaiah, whose writings are found in Isaiah 1—39. He was a poet who predicted the exile but also the return from Babylon. Scholars generally agree that the second part of the book (Isaiah 40—66) was written during or after the exile by a later prophet, or possibly even two. Jeremiah contains history as well as prophecy and tells the story of the last years of the Jewish kingdom. Jeremiah's emphasis was not only on the coming exile but also on the righteousness of God and on the "new covenant," which would be written on the heart. Ezekiel predicted the fall of Jerusalem and the return from exile. His message is one of judgment, but he also offers hope to the exiles with his vision of "a new Jerusalem."

The minor prophets (known in the Hebrew Bible as the "Book of the Twelve") are books that were written by different authors, at different times, and to different audiences. The first six (Hosea, Joel, Amos, Obadiah, Jonah, and Micah) were probably written during the Assyrian occupation (733–650 B.C.); Nahum, Habakkuk, and Zephaniah, during the Babylonian period (663–609 B.C.); and Haggai, Zechariah, and Malachi, during the Persian period and the return from exile (520–430 B.C.). Some prophets were concerned primarily about Israel, the Northern Kingdom: Hosea, Amos (even though he was from the south), and Jonah. Others prophesied in the Southern Kingdom, Judah: Joel, Obadiah, Micah, Nahum, Habakkuk, and Zephaniah.

Although the prophets differ in how they present their message, what they say shows great similarity among them. They describe how Judah and Israel have departed from the covenant and the punishment that will come as a result; but in most cases, they hold out a promise of the restoration that will result from the people's repentance and God's forgiveness. Obadiah, Jonah, and Nahum focus on the sins of Edom and Ninevah, both as a warning to the people of God and as a reminder that God is a universal God who is concerned about other nations as well as the Jews.

Exploration (20 minutes)

Divide the class into six groups. Give each group the name of a prophet and an article on that prophet which you have copied from a Bible dictionary or study Bible. Ask each group to find the following information about their prophet: the name of the king or kings in power at the time of the prophet, the main theme of the prophet's message, and a key verse from the prophet.[6]

Response (10 minutes)

Ask the six groups to share with the class the main themes of their prophets' messages.

Conclusion (10 minutes)

Ask one person from each group to read aloud the key verse selected by the group.

Assignment for Next Time

1. Read Ezekiel 34 and list the feelings the chapter evokes in you.
2. On the outline map provided by the teacher, trace the route of the exile and note the mileage covered.

Basic Biblical Background

Session 9:
The Exile and Return (Ezra–Nehemiah)

Preparation

Make bookmarks for each learner using the prayer from Nehemiah 13:31: "Remember me, O my God, for good."

Opening (10 minutes)

Ask students to close their eyes and imagine what it would be like to be taken suddenly from all that is familiar—home, family, community, church, job—and be forced into exile in another country, unable to return home. Ask the participants to write down as quickly as possible the feelings they think they would have in such circumstances.

Have the class read Psalm 137:1–6. Ask the learners, Does it express feelings similar to yours?

Presentation (15 minutes)

Give a brief lecture covering the following information:

The exile began in 586 B.C., after Jerusalem had passed into Babylonian hands and the Babylonians had implemented their usual policy of deporting captured peoples into their own land. There is not much about the fifty-year period of the exile in scripture, except in Jeremiah, Isaiah (40–66), Ezekiel, and some of the Psalms. But during this period, some important things happened. Judaism took on a new form, centered on the new institution of the synagogue, where people gathered to study the Law, which became its heart and soul. The Israelites began to be known as *Jews,* a word derived from the kingdom of Judah but applied to all of Hebrew descent. The idea of the faithful "remnant" emerges, as well as the understanding of the Messiah as a "suffering servant."

The return to Jerusalem is well documented in the books of Ezra and Nehemiah. It took place in 538 B.C., after Cyrus of Persia overthrew Babylon and issued an edict (found in Ezra 1:2–4 and 6:3–5) ordering the restoration of the Jews to Jerusalem. When they returned under the leadership of Ezra and Nehemiah, they found the city in ruins. The Samaritans living in the land (descendants of Jews who had married people whom the Assyrians had brought from other lands) did not welcome them. The prophets Haggai and Zechariah encouraged the work of rebuilding the Temple in the years 520–515 B.C.

Exploration (15 minutes)

Divide the class into two groups. Ask one group to read the following scripture passages about Ezra and the other to read those about Nehemiah. Then have each group create a brief play about the person assigned to it.

> *Ezra:* Ezra 7:1–20, 25–28; 8:21–23, 31–32, 35; Nehemiah 8:1–3, 5–12
> *Nehemiah:* Nehemiah 1:1–11; 2:1–20; 4:1–6; 6:15–16.

Response (15 minutes)

Let the two groups present their dramas to the whole class.

Conclusion (5 minutes)

Give each learner a bookmark to take home with the prayer of Nehemiah: "Remember me, O my God, for good" (Neh. 13:31). Pray the prayer in unison.

Assignment for Next Time

Review the Gospels and be prepared to tell which is your favorite Gospel and why.

Session 10:
The Gospels (Matthew–John)

Preparation

Prepare a chart, overhead transparency, or handout on the Gospels. (See Appendix, page 123.)

Make copies of the following texts for each student: Matthew 26:20–29; Mark 14:17–25; Luke 22:14–23, John 13:1–30. It is helpful to put the four texts on a page in parallel columns.

Make copies for each student of the worksheet "The Last Supper according to the Gospel Writers." (See Appendix.)

Opening (5 minutes)

Ask the learners to share their favorite Gospel and their reasons for selecting it. Tally on newsprint or chalkboard the "votes" given to each of the Gospels.

Presentation (15 minutes)

Briefly comment on the chart you have prepared about the Gospels, adding other information drawn from your research and reading.

Exploration (20 minutes)

Distribute the worksheets "The Last Supper according to the Gospel Writers." Ask each student to find a partner, and with that partner, answer the worksheet questions.

Response (15 minutes)

Discuss the results of the Gospel comparison exercise on the Last Supper. Ask, What new discoveries did you make?

Conclusion (5 minutes)

Ask class members to share aloud a favorite verse from the Gospels.

Assignment for Next Time

Write the answer to this question: "What can we learn about the early church from Acts 2:37–47?"

Session 11:
The Early Church (Acts)

Preparation

Bring a large map of Paul's missionary journeys for display and discussion. Your church will most likely have such a resource.

Opening (5 minutes)

Ask class members what they learned about the church by reading Acts 2:37–47. List their findings on newsprint or chalkboard.

Presentation (10 minutes)

Give a brief lecture on the following material:

The Acts of the Apostles tells the story of the early church, from its beginnings in Jerusalem to its expansion into the Gentile world and to "the uttermost parts of the earth." It begins with Pentecost and recounts the ministries of Peter, John, Philip, and Stephen but centers on the missionary journeys of Paul, which it describes in detail.

Luke-Acts is actually a two-volume work by the same author. Luke began his Gospel by showing Jesus as the Savior who reached out to strangers and outcasts, and Acts continues that theme by showing God's concern for the whole world, not just the Jews, as the good news spreads among the Gentiles and the church becomes the "new Israel."

Exploration (30 minutes)

Display the map of the geographical area of Paul's journeys.

Divide the class into four groups. Assign one of Paul's journeys, listed below, to each group. Each group should skim the chapters that describe the journey assigned, noting who accompanied Paul and the key incidents that took place on the journey.

> First journey: Acts 13–15:35
> Second journey: Acts 15:36–18:22
> Third journey: Acts 18:23–21:6
> Journey to Rome: Acts 27:1–28:31

When the task is finished, ask the groups to post their notes on the wall and report briefly on their findings.

Response (10 minutes)

Ask the groups to reflect on the notes they have taken, and invite each person to write one line of a prayer of thanksgiving for the church.

Conclusion (5 minutes)

Collect the prayers written by the learners and read them aloud as a closing prayer.

Assignment for Next Time

Choose one of the New Testament epistles and read it through. Be able to give its main theme in one sentence.

Session 12:
The Epistles (Romans–Jude)

Opening (10 minutes)

Ask learners to tell the class which epistle they chose to read and why they chose it.

Basic Biblical Background

Presentation (10 minutes)

Introduce the session with this information:

The letters of Paul address concerns that arose in the early church: issues of theology, discipline, legalism, false teachers, gifts, family relationships, as well as other topics with which the fledgling church struggled in its first century. The church still struggles with many of these issues today. Paul wrote to churches in Rome, Corinth, Galatia, Ephesus, Philippi, Colossus, and Thessalonika, as well as to individuals: Timothy, Titus, and Philemon. These letters were widely circulated and had a great impact on the development of Christian doctrine.

The general epistles are addressed not to specific congregations but to the church at large. Hebrews is actually more a sermon than a letter. Its central theme is that Jesus is both the kingly and priestly Messiah. The epistles of James, Peter, John, and Jude are often called the catholic epistles, meaning that they were intended for the whole world. Like the Gospels, each letter has a different emphasis. James is known as the epistle of works (or ethics), Peter as the epistle of hope, John as the epistle of love, and Jude as the epistle of faith.

Exploration (25 minutes)

Ask the class members to report briefly on the letter they chose, identifying its theme and how it speaks to their own lives. Briefly summarize the letters not chosen. (Use the summary themes below or prepare your own from information in study Bibles or in texts such as *A Bird's-Eye View of the Bible* or *Bible Basics*.)

Themes of the New Testament Epistles

Romans: God's saving righteousness, or justification by faith
1 Corinthians: Unity in the Spirit
2 Corinthians: Paul's concern for the church
Galatians: Justification by faith alone
Ephesians: Unity in Christ to be reflected in the life of the church
Philippians: Persistence in faith in the face of opposition
Colossians: The lordship of Christ
1 Thessalonians: Being steadfast in faith while waiting for Christ's coming
2 Thessalonians: The implications of Christ's return for everyday living
1 Timothy: Order and discipline in the church and opposition to false teachers
2 Timothy: Advice to a young minister on essentials of good leadership

Titus: Requirements of church leaders
Philemon: Showing forgiveness
Hebrews: The priesthood of Christ and the meaning of atonement
James: Living and acting out the gospel
1 Peter: The joys and sufferings of the Christian life
2 Peter: Warnings against false teachers
1 John: God is love
2 John: Love one another
3 John: Extend hospitality
Jude: A warning against division

Response (10 minutes)

Have each learner write a letter to the author of the letter he or she chose, expressing appreciation for specific help the learner received or arguing with the author about some of his points. This can be humorous as well as serious.

Conclusion (5 minutes)

Ask for several volunteers to share their letters.

Assignment for Next Time

Read the Revelation to John and come to the next class with a list of three issues that puzzle you about it and three discoveries you made while reading it.

Session 13:
Revelation

Preparation

Prepare a pasteboard chart, overhead transparency, or handout detailing the symbols most frequently used in apocalyptic writing and their meanings. (See Appendix, p. 126.)

Bring to class colored tissue paper (available in packets of assorted colors at school supply stores and art stores), several small containers of white glue, and construction paper.

Bring several commentaries on Revelation, as well as Bible dictionaries.

Opening (10 minutes)

Begin by asking participants to share the issues and ideas that puzzle them in the book of Revelation. List these on newsprint. On another sheet, list the discoveries they made in their reading.

Presentation (10 minutes)

Deliver brief summary with the following information:

Revelation, also called the Apocalypse, has been a source of fascination, debate, and confusion for centuries. Efforts have long been made to unravel its mysteries and strange symbolic images and use them to predict the future. Revelation is an example of apocalyptic writing, which uses symbolism in the form of numbers, colors, mystical beasts, and upheavals of nature to describe God's government of the whole creation. The book has 275 references to the Old Testament. It was written in apocalyptic "code language" in order to encourage Christians in a time of persecution, to assure them that God "is the ruler yet" and that Christ is triumphant over evil. Revelation is a book about the ultimate victory of God at the conclusion of history, when God's created world will truly become "the kingdom of our Lord and of his Messiah."

Exploration (10 minutes)

Introduce the chart of frequently used apocalyptic symbols as follows:

To untangle apocalyptic writings such as Revelation, it is important to have a clear understanding of the symbols used. Here is a chart of apocalyptic symbols. Other information can be found in books about biblical symbolism or in commentaries on apocalyptic literature.

The learners will doubtless come up with additional questions about Revelation. To help students find answers, provide commentaries and dictionaries and allow time for individual research, so that they can discover answers on their own. Those without further questions may prepare the artwork in the next step. Those who choose to continue researching their questions may do that instead of the art.

Response (15 minutes)

Ask learners to choose a symbol from Revelation and create their own interpretation of it with a tissue-paper collage. Give the following instructions:

Tear the tissue paper to represent the symbol you have chosen, using as many colors as you like. Glue the tissue paper to the construction-paper background sheet. Share your artwork with the class, explaining the meaning of the symbol you have chosen.

Conclusion (15 minutes)

As a conclusion to this segment, ask learners to share a significant discovery they have made about the Bible during the last three months.

4.

Foundations for Faith

THE LANGUAGE OF FAITH

When my husband and I arrived in the Congo in 1957 to begin a term of service as Presbyterian missionaries, our first task was to learn the language of the people. Before we could teach, preach, or even go to the market, it was essential that we be able to communicate our thoughts and ideas. We stumbled at first, of course, and made many mistakes—although none so ludicrous as that of a certain missionary whose error has been used for years to warn new missionaries about the perils of translation. He prayed the Lord's Prayer and used the word for "nose" instead of the word for "heaven" (the two words were spelled the same way but pronounced differently), so that his petition ended up as "Our Father who art in the nose!"

Teaching the faith demands a common language. To do an effective job of traditioning, we must be able to communicate not only stories and images but thoughts and ideas. Those thoughts and ideas make up our belief systems, our doctrines, our theology. Unfortunately, far too many of us have lost the language or never had more than a "pidgin" knowledge of it in the first place. Consequently, we have great difficulty articulating the basic beliefs of the Christian faith and describing the distinctive aspects of our own faith tradition.

The reality is that thousands of Christians today do not really know the meaning of such simple, basic theological terms as *grace, salvation, justification,* and *eternal life.* And yet ministers and teachers go on assuming that when they use such basic terms, everyone is on board. I have a collection of cartoons about heaven and hell. The bizarre theological notions expressed in those cartoons work only because they reflect, in some way, the average person's perceptions. In reality, they are just as far off base as the grotesque medieval images of the afterlife that artists such as Hieronymus Bosch portrayed.

What do we really believe? In an age in which everything is relative and the sharp line between truth and falsehood is increasingly blurred, the question seems unimportant, almost intrusive. Among the most rapidly growing churches are those that stress "community" rather than theological beliefs. People join churches because of their friends or because of the church's proximity to their home. Repeatedly, one hears phrases such as "It really doesn't matter which church you go to; we're all pretty much alike." In the rapidly burgeoning suburban neighborhoods, it is not uncommon to find only 10 or 20 percent of a congregation who have been lifelong members of the denomination to which they now belong.

Does it matter what we believe? Are a blurry "belief in God" and a sketchy "faith in Christ" enough? Many think not. Among them is Robert Browning, editor of *The Pastor as Religious Educator*, who states emphatically:

> In our religious education of persons for the universal priesthood, we must create an atmosphere in which young adults can study the Christian faith as a total system of beliefs in comparison to optional claims and competing philosophies of life so that they can critique the Christian faith freely, rework their earlier ideas and beliefs, and come to an internally meaningful and consistent commitment.[1]

Developing that "internally meaningful and consistent commitment" is actually "doing theology." The word *theology* has acquired something of a bad reputation; it seems to belong in seminaries rather than in our homes. Most Sunday school teachers do not react positively when told they will be teaching theology, but that is exactly what teaching the faith is, whether to two-year-olds or to ninety-year-olds. Even more rare than understanding that teaching the faith is teaching theology is the recognition that struggling patiently and diligently with hard faith questions is "doing theology." Theology is not a dry and boring catalog of doctrines but the stuff of life. It involves the most important questions we can ask, as we try to live lives of faithfulness to God.

It is not enough that a Sunday school teacher's basic purpose is to teach good character, good conduct, or good morals. This kind of character building is no different from that done by many secular agencies and institutions. Religion has a precious treasure to offer, even if it comes in clay pots, and as teachers, we need to be perfectly clear what that treasure is—and then let everyone recognize its value.

The most important prerequisite for teaching faith is having faith. Genuine faith, sincere commitment to God, a knowledge of Jesus Christ, and a desire to grow spiritually are basic requirements for teachers and far more important than having all the answers to doctrinal dilemmas. In fact, when teachers are honest about their own doubts and growing edges, they increase the opportunity for genuine openness and honest searching among class members.

COMMUNICATING THE FAITH

Effective teaching means good communication. How do we communicate through our teaching what the Christian faith is all about? Here are some suggestions:

> Think fearlessly and honestly about all aspects of the faith. Don't be afraid to say, "I'm still struggling with this."
>
> Use words that are easily understood; be simple and clear. Translate theological jargon into everyday words and expressions.
>
> Use the best available teaching tools: curriculum materials, books, visual aids.
>
> Use interactive educational methods, such as discussion, inductive study, creative writing, drama, and art. Don't just lecture and assume your students understand everything. Stimulate them to use their minds.
>
> Rely on the Holy Spirit to provide the final illumination about the truths of the faith, and encourage students to do this as well.

SEGMENT 2: FOUNDATIONS FOR FAITH

Texts

The Bible is the basic text. Remind learners to bring Bibles to each session. Have a few on hand for those who forget.

Each person should have a lay theology textbook for reading assignments. This is an important part of the course. For these sessions, I have chosen Shirley Guthrie's *Christian Doctrine* (Louisville, Ky.: Westminster John Knox Press), which was revised and updated in 1994. Guthrie discusses difficult doctrines in clear and comprehensible terms, delivering them in an inspirational tone that makes them relevant to everyday life.

Guthrie writes from the perspective of the Reformed tradition, although the outline of the book is the Apostles' Creed, an ecumenical statement of faith that nearly all Christians can confess together. If you are from a tradition other than Reformed, you may wish to supplement Guthrie's book with resources from your own denomination that will reflect more sharply your own tradition's theology. Consult your denominational catalogs for books about basic beliefs, written for lay people.

Equipment and Supplies

Ask learners to bring notebooks and pencils and to take notes. Note taking is a valuable way to reinforce learning and provides a helpful future reference for learners.

A flexible seating arrangement is best for breaking into smaller groups. Avoid straight rows of chairs, if possible. Tables for books and notebooks are a real asset. The classroom should be equipped with either newsprint or chalkboard. I prefer newsprint because outlines or comments can be recorded, saved, and referred to later.

Supplies that will be needed for various learning exercises include construction paper, markers, newsprint, clay, scissors, and old magazines. In some cases you will have to prepare worksheets, posters, charts, and mounted pictures before the session.

A Guide to Teaching

Begin each session with prayer, asking for guidance from the Holy Spirit and a willingness to grow mentally and spiritually.

Emphasize the importance of the weekly reading assignments, since those readings form an important part of each session. Add to the information given in these lesson plans additional information from your own reading in Guthrie or in other resources. These plans provide only brief suggestions of content.

Outline of Sessions
1. I Believe in God
2. The Trinity: One God or Three?
3. Maker of Heaven and Earth
4. Providence and Evil
5. The Doctrine of Human Beings
6. Jesus Christ: The Incarnation
7. Jesus Christ: The Atonement and Reconciliation
8. Jesus Christ: The Resurrection
9. The Holy Spirit
10. The Doctrine of Justification
11. The Doctrine of Sanctification
12. The Holy Catholic Church
13. The Life Everlasting

Session 1:
I Believe in God

Preparation

Make a copy of the worksheet "Two Kinds of Revelation" for each student. (See Appendix, page 127.)

From magazines, calendars, and other sources, gather a selection of pictures of nature scenes, families embracing, friends comforting one another, and other subjects that suggest some of God's own characteristics. Mount these on construction paper or lightweight poster board for more stability. Have more pictures than there are class members, so that participants can choose among them.

Make a copy of the Nicene Creed for each student. Many hymnals contain this creed.

Opening (10 minutes)

Welcome the class members and introduce the course in the following manner:

Today we are beginning a study of theology. Although that might sound a little intimidating, it simply means learning about God and God's expectations of us.

Theology is an attempt to take the words of scripture and sort them out in a pattern that gives our lives direction and meaning. We will be discussing themes we have heard about all our lives—justification, forgiveness, redemption, sin—so that we can clarify them and bring them into our everyday lives.

Remember that no one has all the answers about these weighty topics. Together, however, in an atmosphere of trust and openness, we can learn, grow, and gain new insights from one another.

Images are powerful in determining relationship. Our images of who God is and the way in which we relate to God have much to do with our views of and relationships to everything else.

What are some images people have of God? (List the responses on the board or newsprint.) Which images appeal to you most?

Presentation (10 minutes)

Deliver the following presentation:

How do we know there is a God? Through the ages, philosophers and theologians have offered many ways to "prove" God's existence. The idea that there must be a "first cause" that set the universe in motion, the order and intricacy of the created world, and the very existence of a moral law have all been offered as proof that God exists.

Christians believe we get our understanding of God from two kinds of revelation, which we label *general* and *special*. General revelation means that God is revealed in nature, history, and the whole of human life. It places emphasis on such evidences of God as the order and design of the universe, conscience, and the spiritual awareness of a divine presence. Special revelation means the revelation of God through scripture, through the life of Christ, and in the church. It places the emphasis on God seeking us, rather than on our seeking God.

There is a difference between knowing about God and knowing God. To know *about* God is to believe intellectually that there is a God or to possess information about God. To know God is to have a personal experience with God, to acknowledge, confess, honor, thank, and serve God.

Every year polls show that 85 percent of Americans believe that God exists. The question is whether that 85 percent really know God or just know about God.

Exploration (20 minutes)

Distribute the worksheet "Two Kinds of Revelation." (See Appendix, page 127.) Tell learners that to have a clearer understanding of the two kinds of revelation, we will look at what scripture says about God. Ask students to follow the instructions on the worksheet.

Response (15 minutes)

Ask participants to select a picture from the assortment you have prepared and to share with the class what the picture suggests to them about God, as God was revealed in the worksheet readings.

Conclusion: (5 minutes)

Ask the class members to say together the Apostles' Creed.

Assignment for Next Time

1.   Read Guthrie's *Christian Doctrine*, chapter 15.
2.   Distribute copies of the Nicene Creed for each person. Ask the class to answer two questions:
        Which phrases in the creed suggest a unity of Christ and the Holy Spirit with God?
        Which phrases suggest a distinction between God and Christ, God and the Spirit?

Session 2:
The Trinity: One God or Three?

Preparation

Prepare on poster board or overhead transparency the diagram of the Trinity. (See Appendix, page 128.)

Bring an assortment of magazines, old church bulletins, religious advertisements (ask your church office for these), as well as poster paper, scissors, and glue for the poster collages.

Opening (5 minutes)

Divide the chalkboard into three sections or tape three sheets of newsprint to the wall. Label the sections or sheets *Father, Son, Holy Spirit.* Ask the learners, What qualities or characteristics do you associate with the three persons of the Trinity? As the class responds, list the characteristics in the appropriate columns. Do any overlap?

Presentation (10 minutes)

Draw simple pictures on the chalkboard or newsprint of some of the analogies used to explain the Trinity: a three-leafed clover, water/ice/steam, or the sun/the sun's rays/the heat generated by the sun. Explain that none of these analogies is adequate in itself.

Distribute or show on a projector the diagram of the Trinity you have prepared. This illustration demonstrates the unity yet separateness of the three Persons of the Trinity.

Exploration (15 minutes)

Ask learners to read Deuteronomy 6:4. How can this verse be reconciled with the doctrine of the Trinity? Allow learners to share their ideas, then clarify the discussion with these points:

The bottom line of the biblical witness from which any discussion of the Trinity must start is that there is only one God. The confessional statement of Israel—"Hear, O Israel: The LORD is our God; the LORD alone" (Deut. 6:4)— is foundational not only to Judaism but to Christianity as well and was quoted by Jesus as the first and greatest commandment.

Shirley Guthrie says that the Trinity is "a mystery to be confessed, not a mathematical problem to be solved."[2] The mystery is that the three Persons in the Trinity have existed from the beginning. God has always been Father, always Son, always Spirit. In each Person there is unity with God, but each of the Persons is also distinct from the others. One way of expressing the three Persons is to describe the works of God as "Creator, Savior, and Life-renewer," recognizing that *all* of God is involved in *everything* God does.

Question for discussion: What difference does the doctrine of the Trinity make in our lives?

Response (20 minutes)

Provide magazines, old church bulletins, religious advertisements and other collage materials, poster paper, scissors, and glue. Divide the class into three groups, assigning one Person of the Trinity (Father-Creator, Son-Savior, Holy Spirit–Life-renewer) to each group. Ask each group to create a poster collage that illustrates the work of the Person of the Trinity.

Conclusion (10 minutes)

Display the posters made by the groups. Ask for comments on or responses to the collages.

Read the Trinitarian benediction from 2 Corinthians 13:13: "The grace of the Lord Jesus Christ, the love of God, and the communion of the Holy Spirit be with all of you."

Assignment for Next Time

1. Read Guthrie's *Christian Doctrine,* chapter 8.
2. Ask for three volunteers, each of whom will prepare a five-minute presentation for the next class on one of the following: theism, pantheism, and panentheism, using *Christian Doctrine,* pages 153–58 as a reference. Assign the topic and give the volunteers newsprint on which to list the strengths and weaknesses of their assigned topic.

Session 3:
Maker of Heaven and Earth

Opening (10 minutes)

Ask students to list five words that describe God's role as Creator. When they have finished, invite them to share their lists. As they do, write the words on newsprint or chalkboard, underlining those that are duplicated. Ask the class, Are there other words that could be added to define God's role more fully?

Presentation (15 minutes)

In any discussion of how God is related to the created world, a tension arises between the idea of a transcendent God, who is over and above creation, and an immanent God, who is found in creation. Shirley Guthrie identifies three main ways in which Christians in our time talk about God. It is helpful for us to have a clear understanding of the perspectives taken by these three ways—theism, pantheism, and panentheism.

Ask the three learners who volunteered to present their definitions of theism, pantheism, and panentheism.

When the presentations have concluded, ask the class, Which approach seems to you to do the best job of preserving both the transcendence and the immanence of God?

Exploration: (20 minutes)

Discuss the meaning of Genesis 1:31, "It was very good," as interpreted by Guthrie, in *Christian Doctrine*, pages 158–64.

Ask these questions:

> What does it mean to say that all that God has created is good, including human beings?
> What does this have to say about life on this earth?
> What is our responsibility toward the created world?
> What does it mean to have "dominion" over the environment?

Response (10 minutes)

Write a personal creed expressing your beliefs about God as Creator, beginning with "I believe. . . ."

Conclusion (5 minutes)

Ask several students to share their creeds.

Assignment for Next Time

1. Read Guthrie's *Christian Doctrine*, chapter 9.
2. Read Job 38—41, and answer these questions: What was God's answer to Job's question about why good people suffer? Does this satisfy you?

Session 4:
Providence and Evil

Preparation

Make a copy of Psalm 13 for each student.

Opening (10 minutes)

Have the learners discuss times when they may have experienced suffering or heard about suffering that made them ask, "Why do bad things happen to good people?" Allow time for individual responses.

Presentation (15 minutes)

Discuss the homework assignment question about Job. Ask the class to list as many answers as they can give to the question "Where does evil come from?"

Because this is a difficult issue to discuss and understand, you may wish to summarize Guthrie's thoughts in this way:

The Christian faith faces the painful reality of evil head on. From the Fall to the cross, it is evident that our tradition does not try to deny the existence of evil or minimize its power. But it is important to distinguish between two kinds of evil: *natural evil* and *moral evil*.

Karl Barth calls natural evil "the dark side of creation." We hear almost every day of the devastation caused by floods, earthquakes, tornadoes, drought, disease, and accidents. And the question "Why did God let this happen?" always arises. The answer to that question is that they did not happen because God willed. Rather, the world operates according to natural laws that God designed, and the working out of this orderly structure is sometimes beneficial and sometimes harmful to us. The bottom line is that in spite of this "dark side" and in spite of our human finitude that makes death inevitable, God stands by us and is with us to comfort us in our suffering. This is the meaning of the doctrine of providence.

Moral evil, in contrast, is the kind of evil we inflict on one another. It is easy to recognize the enslaving power of evil that makes us do "that which we would not," as even Paul experienced. But God is not the author of evil, so where does evil come from? Some answers that have been given through the ages are: from an evil god who is the rival of the good God; from our own bodily appetites; from unjust social structures. All of these can be refuted. First, there is only one God, so there cannot be an evil god. Second, while our appetites and societies may contribute to evil, they are not its source. Scripture says that evil comes from Satan. Christians differ on whether Satan is a personal devil who literally exists or is a symbolic interpretation of evil; but neither adequately explains the origin of evil. No matter how real the forces of evil, however, we do not believe *in* them so much as *against* them. We believe *in* God, and in God's power to overcome evil.

Exploration (20 minutes)

List the following scripture passages on newsprint or chalkboard:

> Romans 7:14–25
> 2 Corinthians 4:3–4
> Romans 8:37–39
> Colossians 1:11–14
> 1 Corinthians 15:21–28
> 1 John 2:12–14

Divide the class into groups of three. Assign one passage to each group of three. Ask each group to read its passage and answer the questions that follow:

1. What does the passage say about the origin of evil?
2. What does it say is the answer to evil?

Invite the groups to share their answers with the class.

Response (10 minutes)

Distribute copies of Psalm 13 and ask class members to read silently the first four verses. Invite them first to imagine that these words were written by a close friend and then to write a brief note to that friend, offering consolation and hope.

Conclusion (5 minutes)

Ask class members to read in unison Psalm 13:5–6.

Assignment for Next Time

Read Guthrie's *Christian Doctrine*, chapter 10. After reading, finish this sentence: "To be made in the image of God is. . . . "

Foundations for Faith

Session 5:
The Doctrine of Human Beings

Preparation

Make copies for each student of the Apostles' Creed, for the next homework assignment.

Opening (5 minutes)

Describe to the students a cartoon that shows one character saying to another that she is very, very, very, *very* human. Ask your class to respond to these questions: What do you think she was trying to say? Have you ever felt this way? Sometimes we use our "humanness" to excuse our behavior, rather than facing the reality of what being human really means.

Presentation (20 minutes)

Have class members read aloud their homework definitions of what it means to be made in the image of God. As they do so, write the key ideas from each definition on newsprint or chalkboard.

Add to the list these interpretations, if they have not already been identified:

1. To be rational creatures
2. To have a spiritual nature or "soul"
3. To have the ability to make moral judgments
4. To have dominion and power over other creatures
5. To be like Christ
6. To live in total dependence on God, recognizing that everything we have comes from God
7. To accept our role as God's partners, recognizing that we are fully human, endowed with gifts that enable us to participate in God's work
8. To live in community, recognizing that we need and depend on one another for support and care

Ask the group to rank these definitions in importance. Discuss the implications of these responses for how we live our lives.

Exploration (20 minutes)

Write the following questions on newsprint or chalkboard:

1. In what ways can morality be a contradiction of what it means to be human beings in the image of God? (*Christian Doctrine*, p. 195–96.)
2. What can we learn about being a true human being in God's image from the life of Jesus? (*Christian Doctrine*, p. 197–98.)
3. How would you explain the meaning of the statement in Genesis 1:27 that to be created in the image of God is to be male and female? (*Christian Doctrine*, p. 202–4.)

Divide the class into groups of four. Ask each group to discuss the questions, using the indicated pages from *Christian Doctrine* as a resource.

Response (10 minutes)

As the class reassembles, ask this question: "What did you learn from this exercise?" Allow time for several responses.

Conclusion (5 minutes)

Ask learners to join in sentence prayers of confession and praise about being made in God's image. You should begin with the first part of the prayer, inviting the class members to provide the conclusions.

> O God, even though you have made us in your image, we confess that . . . (sentence prayers of confession)
> O God, because you have made us in your image, we praise you . . . (sentence prayers of praise)

Assignment for Next Time

1. Read Guthrie's *Christian Doctrine*, chapter 12.
2. Give each learner a copy of the Apostles' Creed, and ask the class to read carefully the part about Jesus. What phrases about Jesus are the most difficult to understand?

**Session 6:
Jesus Christ: The Incarnation**

Preparation

Gather an assortment of pictures of Jesus. These may be art prints, children's Sunday school teaching pictures, or original interpretations by children or adults. Books of religious art are also good resources.

Foundations for Faith

If students do not bring Bibles to class, make copies of the birth stories in Matthew 1:18–2:23 and Luke 1:26–56; 2:1–10.

Bring a supply of colored construction paper and an assortment of glue bottles.

Opening (10 minutes)

Display the pictures of Jesus around the room. Ask learners to walk around the room, study the pictures, and decide which one speaks to them most clearly of the person of Jesus.

When learners have returned to their seats, ask for volunteers to state which picture they chose and why.

Presentation (15 minutes)

List the questions raised for the class by the Apostles' Creed (homework) on newsprint or blackboard. Keep these in mind throughout this session and the next, and try to address them.

Present a brief summary of the points made in the section "A Real Human Being"(Guthrie, *Christian Doctrine*, p. 237), discussing the issues below and asking the accompanying questions:

1. Docetism is a form of heretical theology that denies Jesus' real humanity. Where do we see docetism practiced in churches today?

2. Jesus was a Jew. What is significant about this fact? Which of the displayed pictures show his Jewishness, and which do not?

3. Jesus experienced every human need and limitation. Do you think Jesus could have thought the earth was flat?

4. Like every human, Jesus was tempted to sin. Nikos Kazantzakis's book *The Last Temptation of Christ* suggests that Jesus was troubled by sexual temptations. Does this bother you? Do you agree with it?

5. Unlike other humans, Jesus was without sin. In what sense was he sinless? What does Guthrie mean when he says, "He was sinless because he was the friend of sinners" (*Christian Doctrine*, p. 241)?

6. Jesus was a dangerous human being. Do you agree with Guthrie that Jesus was offensive socially, politically, morally, and religiously (*Christian Doctrine*, p. 242)?

Exploration (15 minutes)

Read the birth stories in Matthew 1:18–2:23 and Luke 1:26–56; 2:1–10. List all the names or titles given to Jesus. What information do the two stories have in common? What information is unique to each?

Response (15 minutes)

A torn-paper design helps students think through what they have learned. Give each student a sheet of construction paper to use as background. Put paste and many sheets of colored construction paper within easy reach of all students. (No scissors allowed.) Students tear and paste a design on the background that illustrates the humanity of Jesus. The design may be realistic or symbolic.

Conclusion (5 minutes)

Ask students to share their designs with the class.

Assignment for Next Time

1. Read Guthrie's *Christian Doctrine*, chapter 13.
2. Reflect on this statement: "Ancient people believed they could pacify their gods and buy their support by sacrificing animals. How do modern people try to pacify God and win God's approval and help?" Write your answer.
3. Bring your Bible to class next week.

Session 7:
Jesus Christ: The Atonement and Reconciliation

Preparation

Have extra Bibles on hand for those students who do not have them.

Opening (5 minutes)

Write the word *atonement* on newsprint or chalkboard. Ask students to brainstorm ideas or images associated with the word.

Presentation (10 minutes)

Ask students to share their answers to the homework questions. As they do so, list the responses on the chalkboard. Then ask, (1) How do these attempts relate to the ideas about atonement listed on the board? (2) How do they differ from your ideas about atonement?

Offer the following brief summary:

Foundations for Faith

The atonement has been much debated and discussed but still is the object of great confusion in the minds of Christians. Part of the confusion stems from the fact that several images of the atoning death of Christ are given in scripture. Guthrie makes two points about these images: (1) the images serve the event, and (2) no one image is adequate by itself. Each tells us something but not everything. No one image can be pushed too far. We need the various images to get an undistorted picture.

Exploration (30 minutes)

Divide the class into four groups. Assign to each group one of the four biblical images of the atonement discussed in chapter 13 in *Christian Doctrine*. Give the learners the following guidelines for the study of each image:

1. Look up the relevant biblical texts (*Christian Doctrine*, pp. 252–56)

    the slave market (Mark 10:45; 1 Cor. 6:20; 1 Peter 1:18)

    the battlefield (Col. 1:13; 1 Cor. 24—28)

    the sacrificial altar (Mark 14:22–24; John 1:29; Rom. 3:25; 1 Cor. 5:7)

    the courtroom (Rom. 5:6–11; 2 Cor. 5:16–21)
2. What are the advantages of this image in helping us understand the meaning of Jesus' death?
3. What are the limitations of the image?

When the class comes together again, ask for reports on the individual topics. Discuss how the four images together contribute to a full understanding of the atonement.

Response (10 minutes)

Point out to the class that there is no better picture of the reconciling love of God than the parable of the lost son. It describes a love that endures even when it is rejected. Jesus' whole life and teaching had one aim: to reveal and demonstrate that love.

Ask learners to read to themselves the parable in Luke 15:11–32 and then write from the younger son's perspective a description of his feelings.

Conclusion (5 minutes)

Read together Ephesians 2:4–10.

Assignment for Next Time

1. Read Guthrie's *Christian Doctrine*, chapter 14.

2. Compare the versions of the Easter story in Matthew 28:1–20; Mark 16:1–19; Luke 24:1–51; John 20:1–21, 25–27; and 1 Corinthians 15:3–8. Answer these questions:

What is the sequence of events in each story?

How many angels were at the tomb, and where were they?

Who saw the risen Jesus first? In what order did others see him?

What were the reactions of those who saw him? (See *Christian Doctrine*, p. 287.)

Session 8:
Jesus Christ: The Resurrection

Opening (5 minutes)

Post sheets or newsprint or shelf paper on the walls. As students enter, ask them to write on the sheets graffiti-style slogans or expressions describing the meaning of Easter.

Take a few minutes to read aloud some of the expressions.

Presentation (20 minutes)

Begin by asking learners to list the sequence of events in the Gospel resurrection stories. Chart their responses on the chalkboard.

Ask the class, (1) What conclusions would you draw about a comparison of these accounts if you were not a Christian? (2) What are your conclusions as a Christian?

Is it important to believe that the resurrection literally happened? What does Guthrie say about this? (See his response on p. 171 of *Christian Doctrine*: "If it could be said that the whole of the Christian faith stands or falls with any one claim, the claim that God raised the crucified Jesus from the dead is that claim. Without faith in a risen and living Christ there would be no Christianity.")

Exploration (20 minutes)

Divide the class into four groups. Assign to each group one of the four views of the kingdom of God presented in *Christian Doctrine*, pp. 277–87. Ask each group to make a brief summary of that view and report to the class.

Response (10 minutes)

Questions for discussion: Which of the four views of the kingdom of God best describes what you thought about the lordship of Christ before you read this chapter? Have you changed your mind?

Conclusion (5 minutes)

Play a recording of the "Hallelujah Chorus" as a closing meditation.

Assignment for Next Time

1. Read Guthrie's *Christian Doctrine*, chapter 15.
2. List the gifts of the Spirit in 1 Corinthians 12—14.

Session 9:
The Holy Spirit

Preparation

Write each of the following passages in full on a separate index card: Genesis 1:2; Genesis 2:7; Psalm 104:30; Exodus 31:1–6; Job 32:8; Isaiah 11:1–5; Isaiah 61:1–4.

Bring to class enough potter's clay so that each student will have a lump about four inches square. Potter's clay is found in art stores or teachers' supply stores. If you cannot find the real thing, use Play-Doh or modeling clay, but they are poor substitutes for the real thing.

Opening (5 minutes)

On the blackboard or on newsprint, write this question: "Is the Spirit more likely to be present in the church sanctuary or in a church classroom?"

After giving class members time to reflect silently on the question, ask for a show of hands for each option and tally the responses on the blackboard or newsprint. Then open the discussion by asking why class members felt as they did.

Presentation (15 minutes)

Distribute the prepared index cards to seven students. Tell them you are going to read several sentences (given below) that describe the work of the Spirit of God in the Old Testament. When a scripture passage matches a description, the student is to read that passage aloud.

1. The Spirit is at work in God's creation and preservation of the world and human life.

2. The Spirit of God is the source of human culture, art, creativity, and wisdom.
3. The Spirit of God is on the side of all who are helpless, poor, wretched, and oppressed.

Exploration (20 minutes)

Ask class members to name the gifts of the Spirit they found in reading 1 Corinthians 12—14. List the gifts on newsprint or chalkboard.

Class members should form pairs to discuss the following questions about the list of gifts:

Why are the gifts given?
Do they conflict with one another?
Do all Christians receive the same gifts?
What is the greatest gift?
What does Paul think of "speaking in tongues"?

Response (15 minutes)

Give each learner a lump of potter's clay. Ask learners to make a symbolic representation of the Holy Spirit. Group the completed representations on a table, and allow time for all to view them and ask questions of the creators.

Conclusion (5 minutes)

As a closing prayer, read the words of the hymn "Come, Holy Spirit, Heavenly Dove."

Assignment for Next Time

Read Guthrie's *Christian Doctrine*, chapter 16. Then answer this question in twenty words or less: "What is faith?" Bring your written answer to class.

Session 10:
The Doctrine of Justification

Opening (10 minutes)

Invite class members to turn to the person next to them and share their answers to the homework question "What is faith?"

Foundations for Faith

Presentation (15 minutes)

Summarize briefly the following points from chapter 16 of *Christian Doctrine:*

1. Justification by faith was a basic theme of the Reformation.
2. We do not have to save ourselves by being good.
3. God's love is a free gift; we cannot buy it.
4. God already loves us and accepts us, even though we are sinners.
5. God's love justifies us, making things right between us and God.
6. Neither our good works nor our faith justifies us.
7. God alone justifies us, by grace in Christ.
8. Faith does not save us; it is our way of acknowledging that we are saved.

Exploration (20 minutes)

Ask learners to read Paul's doctrine of justification in Rom. 3:21–26 and compare his statement with Jesus' parable in Luke 18:10–14. Allow five to ten minutes for this, then ask the following questions:

> Does Jesus' story help you understand what Paul was talking about? In what ways?
> Who does the Pharisee represent?
> Who does the tax collector represent?

Response (10 minutes)

Ask learners to create a five-line acrostic poem, using the five letters of the word *FAITH* to begin each line. The poem does not have to rhyme, and if they cannot think of a word, phrase, or sentence to follow a letter, learners should simply go on to the next line. They will be asked to share only one line rather than the whole acrostic. When everyone is finished, call out the letter and let all who wish to share their line do so. Then move on to the next letter.

Conclusion (5 minutes)

Ask for sentence prayers of thanksgiving for God's free grace.

Assignment for Next Time

1. Read Guthrie's *Christian Doctrine,* chapter 17.

2. Read the Sermon on the Mount (Matt. 5—7). Be ready to discuss this question: "Do you think we should take its commands literally?"

Session 11:
The Doctrine of Sanctification

Opening (10 minutes)

We cannot talk about the doctrine of sanctification without talking about holiness, because the verb *to sanctify* means "to make holy."

Ask the class, When you hear the word *holy*, what comes into your mind? List their answers on newsprint or a chalkboard.

Presentation (5 minutes)

Explain that the root meaning of the word *holy* is "separate" or "different." As children of God, we are called to live "holy" lives, although very few people are comfortable with that term. From the life of Jesus and in the biblical witness, we learn that a life of holiness involves self-denial and cross bearing. As God's "holy people" we are different, and often that means confrontation with the world. Jesus describes that "differentness" in the Sermon on the Mount. In this session, we will explore Jesus' holiness, or differentness.

Exploration (30 minutes)

Divide the class into three groups, assigning each group a chapter of the Sermon on the Mount. Each group should list what Christ asks of his followers, and as they do this, put a check by those that are doable and a cross by those that seem impossible or impractical.

Before the groups begin work, present Guthrie's guidelines for interpreting Jesus' sayings:

1. Remember that Jesus spoke always to particular people in particular situations. All people are not required to do things in the same way.
2. Although we cannot make a set of rules out of Jesus' commands, we must try to discover what it means to echo his attitude faithfully and obediently in our everyday lives.
3. Jesus demands a costly nonconformity but also brings freedom from enslaving loyalties to the world and freedom for God and others.

When they have finished their lists, ask the groups to make brief oral summaries of their findings. Allow plenty of time for discussing how we are to live out Jesus' commands. (For helpful questions to guide the discussion, see *Christian Doctrine*, p. 347.)

Response (15 minutes)

Ask learners to pretend they just heard Jesus speak these words from Matthew 5—7. Have each learner write a letter to Jesus, telling him how he or she intends to put into practice his commands.

Conclusion

Pray together the Lord's Prayer.

Assignment for Next Time

1. Read Guthrie's *Christian Doctrine,* chapter 18.
2. Consider this question: "Why do you need the church?" List as many answers as you can.

Session 12:
The Holy Catholic Church

Opening (5 minutes)

Invite students to write, as quickly as possible, the words or phrases that come to mind when they hear the word *church*. Give them one minute to do this, then ask them to share aloud their words.

Presentation (10 minutes)

Begin with these or similar introductory remarks:

What is the church? Where is the church? There is no mention of church buildings in the New Testament. Early Christians met in private homes. Only twice is the term *church* used in the four Gospels (Matt. 16:18; 18:17), but several times Jesus said to the group of disciples, "You are . . . ," using a word image rather than an abstract definition of what the members of his church are called to be. For example, in the Sermon on the Mount, he said, "You are the salt of the earth" (Matt. 5:13) and "You are the light of the world" (Matt. 5:14). Similarly, Paul and other New Testament writers used images rather than definitions to suggest who the church is and what its members are commissioned to do.

Exploration (25 minutes)

Explain that there are at least ninety-six images for the church in the New Testament. In the short time we have, we will be able to explore only a few of them.
List the following passages on the board or newsprint:

Matthew 5:13	2 Corinthians 3:3
Matthew 5:14	2 Corinthians 3:18
John 10	2 Corinthians 5:20
John 15	Ephesians 2:19
1 Corinthians 3:9	Ephesians 5:25–32
1 Corinthians 3:16	2 Timothy 2:5
1 Corinthians 12:27	1 Peter 2:9

Divide the class into groups of three to five people. Provide each group with a large sheet of paper and markers. The assignment for each group is (1) to look for images for the church in the passages above and (2) to make simple line drawings of each image on the sheet, adding the scripture reference below the drawing.

Post the sheets of illustrations on the wall.

Response (10 minutes)

Ask each class member to discuss with another person this question: "What do these images say to you about the life and mission of the church?"

Conclusion (10 minutes)

Ask learners to complete this sentence in writing: "The mission of the church in the world is to. . . ." Invite several participants to share their sentences aloud.

Assignment for Next Time

1. Read Guthrie's *Christian Doctrine*, chapter 19.
2. Each learner should ask two people *not* in the class the question "What is your idea of heaven?" and bring their answers to the next class.

Session 13:
The Life Everlasting

Preparation

Bring an assortment of magazines, glue, and several sheets of newsprint.

Foundations for Faith

Opening (10 minutes)

Invite the class to share the ideas of heaven they collected from their conversations. After everyone has shared, ask the class, What do these comments suggest to you? Are there any you disagree with?

Presentation (20 minutes)

Tell the class that you are giving a true-or-false test on information found in chapter 19 of *Christian Doctrine*. They should number a sheet of paper from 1 to 10 and write "True" or "False" for each of the following statements you read. (The correct answers are in parentheses.)

1. The Christian hope for individuals is hope for our own resurrection. (T)

2. The Christian hope for the world is that God will create a new heaven and a new earth. (T)

3. The justice, freedom, and peace of the kingdom of God will be brought about as a result of human efforts. (F) (Correct answer: The kingdom of God will come at the end of history as the result of what only God can and will do. See *Christian Doctrine*, p. 375.)

4. When we look around at the massive suffering and injustice we experience in our own lives and in the world around us, we realize it is hopeless to try to alleviate that suffering. (F) (Correct answer: For Christians to fall into such hopelessness is sin, a lack of faith and hope in the triune God they confess. See *Christian Doctrine*, p. 376.)

5. What happens at death is that our bodies die but we ourselves live on and return to the spiritual realm from which we came and to which we really belong. (F) (Correct answer: This is unacceptable from a biblical point of view, which holds that the soul is not the divine part of us but simply the breath of life. It is as mortal as our bodies. See *Christian Doctrine*, p. 379.)

6. The Bible says that death is not so bad after all because we do not actually die. (F) (Correct answer: In the Bible, death is real, total, and dreadful. Our hope is not in our ability to overcome the power of death but in God's ability to make the dead live again. See *Christian Doctrine*, p. 380.)

7. In the Old Testament, everyone who dies goes to the same place, Sheol, where the dead have a shadowy kind of existence. (T)

8. The Bible's description of hell as a place of fire is to be taken literally. (F) (Correct answer: Biblical language about the future is metaphorical or symbolic. For the people of Jesus' time, fire was a symbol of the destruction of everything displeasing to God. See *Christian Doctrine*, p. 383.)

9. The last judgment will come as good news for everyone. (T) (See *Christian Doctrine*, pp. 387–88.)

10. We look forward to a future in which we, the bodily creaturely persons we are now, will live in communion with God and other people. (T)

Review the statements with the class and give the correct answers. Allow for questions and discussion as you proceed.

Exploration (10 minutes)

Give the following directions:

Gather in groups of three or four. Choose one person to read aloud 1 Corinthians 15:35–50 and 1 John 3:2; then discuss these questions: "What does Paul think our resurrected bodies will be like?" "Does the verse from John help with this question?" "What is your idea of the resurrected body?"

Response (15 minutes)

Ask students to read silently the section "We Will All Live in the City" (*Christian Doctrine*, pp. 390–91).

Have the students, working in groups of four or five, select magazine pictures to make a collage that illustrates symbolically the city of God. They should paste the pictures to a sheet of newsprint. Each group should explain its collage briefly to the class.

Conclusion (5 minutes)

Ask one learner to read the "warning" on p. 397 of *Christian Doctrine*, and another to read the "promise" on p. 398.

5.

Timely Teaching Tips

Christa McAuliffe, the teacher who died in the *Challenger* space shuttle explosion, is widely quoted as saying, "I touch the future . . . I teach." Nowhere is this more true than in the process of teaching the faith. The responsibility is a huge and joyous one, enormously satisfying, unendingly challenging, never adequately done but nevertheless the source of amazing miracles.

For as long as I can remember, I have loved teaching. It has been the dessert of my life, a sweetness that is both satisfying and energizing. I love the interaction of mutual discovery, the challenge of exploring puzzling paradoxes, the layering of experience and texts that somehow, mysteriously, glimpse truth. But I have learned the hard way that teaching is not one-sided. It is not a matter of saturating the brains of others with one's accumulated wisdom. Instead, it is listening and allowing and learning—as well as informing and sharing—so that true traditioning can take place.

The balance between careful preparation and classroom flexibility is crucial to maintain but not always easy. The teacher needs a game plan, needs to have thought through goals and purposes, and needs to have searched out the very best methods to achieve those goals. Good teaching is a never-ending search for ways of communicating ideas that not only inform but will motivate learners and get their creative and interpretive juices flowing.

HELPFUL RESOURCES

This chapter provides a series of lesson plans on the principles and methods of good teaching and learning. In addition to these lesson plans, I recommend that you consult other resources for additional creative ideas on teaching.

I have found the following books helpful in my own teaching. At this writing, all are in print.

Mary Duckert, *Help! I'm a Sunday School Teacher*, rev. ed. (Louisville, Ky.: Westminster John Knox Press, 1995). Emphasizes methods that are appropriate to different teaching and learning styles.

Donald L. Griggs, *Basic Skills for Church Teachers* (Nashville: Abingdon Press, 1985). An excellent workbook on teaching, with emphasis on developing Bible skills.

Donald L. Griggs, *Teaching Teachers to Teach: A Basic Manual for Church Teachers* (Nashville: Abingdon Press, 1980). A how-to book for teachers on lesson planning, leading discussions, and other aspects of teaching. Very helpful for teachers of adults.

Roberta Hestenes, *Using the Bible in Groups* (Philadelphia: Westminster Press, 1985). A superb guide to inductive Bible study for adults.

Richard Rusbuldt, *Basic Teacher Skills*, rev. ed. (Valley Forge, Pa.: Judson Press, 1997). Excellent, down-to-earth suggestions about session planning, teaching activities, and so forth.

SEGMENT 3: TIMELY TEACHING TIPS

Preparation

The sessions in this segment provide hands-on experience in the methods being considered. Each session uses the parable of the prodigal son in Luke 15:11–32 to demonstrate many different ways of teaching one passage. I recommend that you find as many pictures of this parable as you can. Look in art books, Sunday school teaching packets, and portfolios of art prints. Keep the pictures on display during the entire segment.

The sessions in this segment demand careful advance preparation by the teacher: setting up the room in the best arrangement possible for the type of session that is planned; making sure all the supplies needed for the learning activities are on hand; and preparing the handouts, worksheets, or charts that accompany the sessions. You will need to have on hand the following art supplies: newsprint, markers, clay, paints, glue, scissors, and construction paper. Arrange for equipment such as slide projectors, tape recorders, and overhead projectors when necessary. As you develop ideas throughout the sessions, you may identify additional materials.

At the first class, request that all learners come to class with Bibles and notebooks and take notes. Remind them that note taking is an excellent way to reinforce learning.

At the end of each session, ask class members to review the methods that have been used in the course. This will help make them more sensitive to what they are experiencing in the classroom.

A Guide to Teaching

Begin each session with prayer, asking for guidance from the Holy Spirit and a willingness to grow mentally and spiritually. Regularly emphasize the importance of the homework assignments, since each contributes substantially to the next session.

Outline of Sessions

1. The Purpose of Christian Education
2. Growing in Faith
3. The Learning Environment
4. Preparing to Teach
5. The Nonboring Lecture
6. Storytelling
7. How to Lead Discussions
8. Inductive Bible Study
9. Using Drama to Teach
10. Learning Centers for All Ages
11. Creative Writing
12. Teaching with Art
13. Summary Session

Session 1:
The Purpose of Christian Education

Preparation

Make a copy for each student of 2 Timothy 3:14–17.

Opening (10 minutes)

Ask the class, What do you think is the purpose of Christian education? Write the responses on newsprint or a chalkboard.

Presentation (10 minutes)

Introduce the session with the following summary of ideas, found more fully in chapter 1 of this book. (Refer to chapter 1 if necessary.)

Church educators have always debated among themselves about the primary purpose of Christian education. Some have emphasized instruction, others becoming part of the faith community, others spiritual development, and still others education for justice and social change. Recent years have seen the emergence of a new emphasis on Christian education as "traditioning," passing on the meaning of the faith community from one generation to the next. This is a task of both the home and the church.

Traditioning both *binds* and *reminds*. It binds members of the faith community by providing a common language through which the heritage of the community is claimed. It reminds us that we are a part of that community which gives us meaning. We tell the "old, old story" so that future generations will know who they are. Traditioning is necessary for the survival of any institution. The fundamental ideals and purposes of the institution must be not only understood clearly but passed on to succeeding generations.

The implications are clear. Teachers in the church have an extremely important and precious task: that of traditioning, of passing on to the generations to come the story of what it means to be God's people.

The purpose of Christian education is not to fill people's heads with biblical trivia. It is to tell the family story, that story we find in scripture, with such imagination and verve that lives are illuminated and changed. It is a heavy responsibility. It requires knowledge of both the biblical story and how to interpret it. It requires skill in storytelling and good communication techniques. It demands sympathetic understanding of both the biblical text and the context in which the learners live. When the story is told in a way that engages people's lives, community is formed, spiritual growth occurs, and people are moved to work for social justice and change.

Exploration (20 minutes)

Scripture clearly understands the importance of traditioning. It takes place in many ways and in many settings. By looking at some of these ways of traditioning, we will have a clearer understanding of its importance.

Divide the class into groups of two or three. Assign one of the passages below to each group.

Exodus 18:13–23	Matthew 5:1, 19; 11:1
Deuteronomy 4:5–14	Mark 4:1–12
Deuteronomy 6:4–9, 20–25	Mark 6:1–6
Deuteronomy 32:44–47	Acts 5:17–21, 25–29, 40–42
Ezra 7:25–26	1 Timothy 4:11–16
Psalm 78:1–8	2 Timothy 1:3–14
Ezekiel 44:15–24	2 Timothy 4:1–5

Give the groups these questions to answer:

> What does the passage say about the importance of traditioning?
> How is it to be done?
> What will be the result?

Response (15 minutes)

Ask groups to share their answers to the questions with the class.

Conclusion (5 minutes)

Read in unison 2 Timothy 3:14–17.

Assignment for Next Time

Divide a sheet of paper into eight columns. Label each column with one of these age groups: ages 2–3, 4–6, 7–11, 12–14, 15–18, 19–30, 31–55, 55 and over. Write as many characteristics of each age group as you can think of in each column.

Session 2:
Growing in Faith

Preparation

Bring eight sheets of newsprint, eight markers, and masking tape.
Make copies of the handout "Age-Appropriate Learning Activities." (See Appendix, page 129.)

Opening (5 minutes)

As we teach, we must always take into consideration the characteristics of the persons in the age group we are teaching. Their spiritual and psychological needs, physical abilities, and mental capacities all affect the methods we use in teaching. Today we will reflect together about the characteristics of various age groups and some teaching activities appropriate for each.

Presentation (25 minutes)

Present the following information:
Each of us knows what it is like to be a child, a teenager, and an adult. In your homework assignment, you drew on that experience, as well as your experiences of being parents, grandparents, siblings, and teachers, to think about the characteristics of the following eight age groups: nursery (2–3), preschool (4–6),

elementary (7–11), early adolescence (12–14), youth (15–18), young adults (19–30), middle adults (31–55), and older adults (over 55). I now invite you to pool your collective wisdom to come up with a definitive list of characteristics.

Divide the class into eight small groups, assigning to each group one of the eight age categories. Give each small group a sheet of newsprint and a marker. They have ten minutes to write down as many characteristics as possible of that age group. At the end of the ten minutes, ask the groups to tape their lists to the wall. (If your class is too small to divide into eight groups, assign more than one category to each group.)

Read each list aloud. Make sure that the following characteristics are included, and add them if they are not.

Nursery
Highly active, eager to learn but have short attention span, learn best by doing, independent, like to play alone, enjoy hearing stories and videos over and over, learning to trust. Need to feel safe and accepted in the church and to know that God loves them and cares for them.

Preschool
Energetic, literal-minded, self-centered, imaginative, limited sense of time and space, can experience real worship. Need to know the church as the place to be with God and to think of God as One on whom they can rely.

Elementary
Curious, active, imaginative, understand cause and effect, beginning to establish self-identity. Need to learn about the persons and stories of the church and its covenant and mission and to develop an assurance of God's care and forgiveness.

Early adolescence
Maturing physically, peer group very important, want to be heard and included, enjoy challenges, can reason and discuss. Need to understand the church as an agency of God and to know they are the children of God and are loved by God.

Youth
Seeking identity, egocentric, can do abstract thinking, capable of intense loyalties, self-conscious, easily embarrassed, want to perform well, anxious to fulfill expectations of significant authority figures. Need to know and understand the faith tradition, to develop a theology of the church, to feel loved and forgiven by God, and to trust in God's will.

Young adults

Idealistic; making major decisions about work, marriage, and lifestyle; altruistic; like to support causes; leaving "home," physically and emotionally; searching for values. Need to understand the importance of the church as a faith community to which they belong and to think of God as "true home."

Middle adults

Settling down, sensitive to community and political responsibilities; developing skills and abilities under stress and pressure; trying to convert dreams into reality. Need to identify the church as a community working for justice and compassion for others and to hear God's call to them to become involved in that work.

Older adults

Experiencing retirement anxiety and physical limitations; adjusting to the empty nest; less willing to experiment; increased dependence on others; great need for companionship; more time for leisure, hobbies, travel, and church. Need to experience the church as a family bound together in a common covenant and to trust in God as a source of strength, renewal, and comfort.

Exploration (10 minutes)

Distribute copies of "Age-Appropriate Learning Activities." (See Appendix, page 129.) Ask the class to read the list over and think of one method for each group that would be appropriate for teaching the parable of the prodigal son in Luke 15:11–32.

Response (15 minutes)

When the participants have completed the task, invite them to share their ideas aloud. Suggest that other class members take notes of the ideas presented.

Conclusion (5 minutes)

Listen to these words from Paul to Timothy about the rewards of good teaching, and be inspired by them: "Pay close attention to yourself and to your teaching; continue in these things, for in doing this you will save both yourself and your hearers" (1 Tim. 4:16).

Assignment for Next Time

Talk to someone who teaches in the church and ask him or her these questions:

1. What physical facilities are necessary for learning for all ages?
2. What special physical facilities are necessary for your class? (Note the age level of class.)

Session 3:
The Learning Environment

Opening (10 minutes)

Ask class members to share the observations they gathered in their homework interviews. Are there any generalizations that can be made from the responses teachers gave to the questions?

Presentation (15 minutes)

Give the following presentation:

The importance of the physical learning environment cannot be overstated. Seating arrangements can help or hinder discussion. Noises from outside can be distracting. Messy, dirty rooms with out-of-date posters and announcements adorning the bulletin boards give the impression that nobody cares. A lack of writing or display equipment, such as bulletin boards, chalkboards, and newsprint, handicaps interactive learning. Even temperature matters—if students are uncomfortably hot or cold they don't concentrate well.

In his book *To Know as We Are Known*, educator Parker Palmer emphasizes the importance of creating a learning space with openness yet boundaries and with a sense of hospitality. One way this can be accomplished, he says, is in the physical arrangement of the classroom. When chairs are arranged in straight rows facing the teacher, he maintains, it creates a space "in which there is no room for students to relate to each other and each other's thoughts . . . but when chairs are placed in a circle, creating an open space between us, within which we can connect, something else is said. The teacher may sit in that circle and talk, but we are all being invited to create a community of learning by engaging the ideas and one another in the open space between."[1]

Circles of chairs are not the only room arrangement possible. There are times when a theater-type arrangement is preferable, or when students should be grouped around tables or in semicircles. If several activities are being offered during a class, as in the learning center approach, worktables or centers need to be arranged with sufficient space for moving among them. The important thing is to choose a room arrangement that suits the format of the session, rather than remaining with the same setting you inherited from a previous teacher.

Another important aspect of learning is the use of teaching pictures, posters, charts, and maps. It seems to be a fixed idea in most churches that only children need these. But adults learn visually as well and can profit enormously from well-chosen pictures that both inspire and edify.

What can you do if you have little space? Small churches and churches whose rooms are used as day-care centers often face this problem. Here are a few suggestions:

1. Use the sanctuary as a classroom. This is often done for adults, but it works for children and youth too. Instead of seating them formally in the pews, however, let them sit on the floor on carpet squares or small rugs. The pews can be used for displays and flip charts. Students can use lapboards or clipboards for writing.
2. When buying new tables, look for tables that permit versatile grouping, for instance, trapezoidal ones or those with folding legs.
3. If your classroom space has no bulletin boards for displays, make simple easels cut from the corners of boxes, or make portable bulletin boards like folding screens.

Invite class members to contribute other space-saver ideas they have used or experienced.

Exploration (20 minutes)

Divide the class into groups of four. Supply each group with a teacher's guide and learner's book from old curriculum materials.

Ask the groups to choose one of the lessons in the curriculum material and to draw a diagram of the physical setting that would best facilitate learning. Ask them to note what special equipment, work space, display space, and seating will be needed.

When the groups have completed this work, ask them to share their diagrams and ideas with the whole class.

Response (10 minutes)

On the chalkboard, draw diagrams of Room A (chairs arranged facing a lectern, row upon row) and Room B (chairs placed in a circle and an open space in the middle).

Ask learners to reflect on the two learning environments by completing the following statements:

"As a student in Room A, I feel. . . . "
"As a student in Room B, I feel. . . . "

Conclusion (5 minutes)

Ask for volunteers to read aloud their reflections.

Assignment for Next Time

Ask learners to write the answers to the following questions:

1. Which three persons were outstanding teachers in your life before you were fifteen?
2. Which three persons have been outstanding teachers in your life as an adult?
3. What leads you to remember them as outstanding?[2]

Session 4:
Preparing to Teach

Preparation

Make a copy for each student of "Guidelines for Preparing to Teach." (See Appendix, page 131.)
Make a copy of Luke 15:11–32 for each student.

Opening (10 minutes)

Ask students to share their homework and identify the qualities of outstanding teachers. As they do so, write the qualities on newsprint or a blackboard.

Presentation (15 minutes)

Introduce the topic, using the following paragraph as a basis for your discussion:

Nothing is more essential to good teaching than good preparation. The teachers whom you have described as outstanding undoubtedly recognized that fact. If teachers are serious about their "call to teach," then they have a responsibility to their students: the responsibility of being well prepared. Being prepared does not mean having all the answers. It does not mean allotting a half hour on Saturday night to "going over the lesson" in the teacher's guide. It does not mean yielding to the inertia of using the same old methods Sunday after Sunday, regardless of what the teacher's guide suggests.

Next, distribute copies of "Guidelines for Preparing to Teach " (See Appendix, page 131.)

Exploration (20 minutes)

Ask students to imagine they are to teach the parable of the prodigal son (Luke 15:11–32) to a class of twelve-year-olds. Distribute to each student the scripture passage you copied earlier. Give them the following assignment:

1. Identify the key concept of the lesson.
2. Plan a way to open the session.

Invite class members to share their responses aloud. Then, ask the whole class to brainstorm teaching methods that would be effective for twelve-year-olds in the other four key parts of the session (presenting, exploring, responding, and concluding). They can refer to their notes on appropriate methods for early adolescents.

Response (10 minutes)

Ask each student to discuss this question with one other person in the class: "How does careful planning help in the task of building up the body of Christ to glorify God and serve one's neighbor?"

Conclusion (5 minutes)

Ask the class to share, "popcorn style" (meaning quickly and at random), their answers to the question just discussed.

Assignment for Next Time

Write down three reasons you like the lecture method of teaching and three reasons you do not like it.

Session 5:
The Nonboring Lecture

Preparation

Print on a separate sheet of newsprint the following quote:

Never, never, never lecture, unless there is no other way to help persons learn. *Search, search, search* for other ways first, then, if there is no other way, the lecture is for you.—Martha Leypoldt

Opening (10 minutes)

Ask learners to share and discuss the reasons they like the lecture method. List them on a chalkboard. Then do the same thing with the reasons they do not like lectures.

Presentation (15 minutes)

Give the following lecture, showing the quotation on newsprint as you read it:

In her excellent book on teaching *Learning Is Change*, Martha Leypoldt gives an emphatic rule, especially important for teachers of adults: "*Never, never, never* lecture, unless there is no other way to help persons learn. *Search, search, search* for other ways first, then, if there is no other way, the lecture is for you."[3]

The lecture method is preferred by many teachers, but studies have shown that lecturing is the least effective way of teaching. We retain only 10 percent of what we hear. Although lecturing may be the quickest and easiest method for the teacher, it is the least interesting for the student. In this session, we look at five problems with lecture methods and identify six basic guidelines for using the lecture effectively.

Five Problems with Lecturing

1. It increases dependency and passivity on the part of learners. Lecture has been described as the easiest method for both teacher and student. It is easiest for the teacher because the teacher is in control of both subject matter and process. It is easiest for the students because they simply absorb what is handed out and do not have to become involved with the subject or do much real thinking about it.

2. Lecture is predictable. There are no surprises. The teacher talks. The students listen. No unexpected demands are made by the teacher of the student or the student of the teacher. This can be dreary and boring for the student.

3. Once it is turned on, it is hard to turn off. The lecture method is particularly favored by authoritarian personalities who like the sound of their own voices but are not particularly interested in hearing the students' points of view. When students ask questions, the questions precipitate another ten minutes of lecture, rather than being a true discussion.

4. Students may not be learning as much as you think they are. Just because they are listening does not mean any real growth or change has taken place.

5. Lecture often engages only the students' ears and not their whole minds. The students' creative thoughts and ideas are not given voice.

Basic Guidelines for Lecturing

1. Remember that the purpose of the lecture is to inform, explain, compare, and summarize.

2. In terms of content, concentrate on what is relevant and important. Be guided by your audience. Determine their level of comprehension.

3. Be well prepared; know what you are talking about. Outline at the beginning what you will talk about, then present the information, and end by summarizing. Remember the old saying, "Tell 'em what you're going to tell 'em; tell 'em; tell 'em what you told 'em."

4. Use the very best grammar, diction, and vocabulary possible. Use vivid examples and illustrations. Speak with clarity and energy. Root out mannerisms and clichés.

3. Be passionate and enthusiastic about the information you are imparting. Convey that enthusiasm through body language and voice.

4. Use visual resources: outlines on chalkboard, information already written on overhead transparencies or newsprint, posters, maps, pictures, charts, illustrative objects, handouts.

5. Assume that learners want to learn. Remember that you are not teaching information as much as you are teaching people. Don't think of it as "filling empty heads with knowledge." Think of it as actively engaging learners in an exciting exploration of new ideas and material. Engage them with your questions and provide opportunities for theirs. Allow time for their response to your input.

6. Keep it short. End on time. Leave them hungry for more.

Exploration (20 minutes)

Divide the class into groups of three. Ask each group to create an outline for an informational lecture on the parable of the prodigal son. They should consider what kind of information should be included in a lecture on this passage (for example, the definition of a parable).

Reconvene the group and share each group's outlines with the class.

Response (5 minutes)

Ask students to write and complete the following sentence in their notebooks: "In the future, I will try to rely less on the lecture method because. . . . "

Conclusion (10 minutes)

Close with the following litany of confession:

> For the insecurity that makes us want to appear to have all the answers,
> *O Lord, forgive us.*
> For our unwillingness to take risks,
> *O Lord, forgive us.*
> For our reluctance to respect the insights of others,
> *O Lord, forgive us.*
> For loving the sound of our own voices too much,
> *O Lord, forgive us.*
> In the name of the Master Teacher, Amen.

Assignment for Next Time

In the next class, be able to tell the parable of the prodigal son as if it took place in contemporary times.

Session 6:
Storytelling

Preparation

Cut a long strip of newsprint about six inches wide for each student. Bring a supply of felt-tip markers, one or two for each student.

Opening (5 minutes)

As an example of powerful storytelling, read to the class James Weldon Johnson's poem "The Prodigal Son" from his collection *God's Trombones.* (You can find this in your public library.)

Presentation (10 minutes)

Introduce today's session in this way:

Timely Teaching Tips

Stories are extremely important in the traditioning process. The Old Testament contains many stories that were part of the oral tradition of Israel and of the way in which the Israelites defined who they were. Storytelling is a great method to use with youth and adults as well as with children. Even if you have not had much experience with storytelling, there are ways to improve your skills. Here are some suggestions:

1. Start a story file, sorting stories by categories, such as faith, friendship, family ties, grief, joy. When you hear or read a good story or illustration, place it in the file under the proper heading.
2. Record your voice as you read or tell stories. Listen for stammering or frequent use of filler expressions such as "uh."
3. Make eye contact with listeners.
4. Let your voice reflect emotions.
5. Use pauses for emphasis.
6. Use appropriate gestures.
7. Do not conclude a story with a moral but invite responses to the story with discussions, artwork, puppets, acting out the story, songs.

Exploration (20 minutes)

Ask class members to tell their version of the parable of the prodigal son to one other person, and have that person give feedback about the presentation. Then change roles so the other person has a turn. Each person should take about five minutes to tell his or her story, allowing five minutes for the feedback.

Response (15 minutes)

One method to encourage careful listening to stories is a form of "doodling." Give each person a long strip of newsprint and markers. As you read the parable of the prodigal son, they should draw on their strips doodles, some kind of symbolic or representative drawing that suggests what is happening in the story and the emotions the persons in the parable may have had.

Conclusion (10 minutes)

Ask for volunteers to show their strips, interpreting them to the class.

Assignment for Next Time

Be prepared to discuss the parable of the prodigal son in Luke 15:11–32. Read the text again slowly and thoughtfully, then read a commentary on the passage. Two good ones are *Luke,* by Fred Craddock (Interpretation series; Louisville, Ky.: Westminster John Knox Press, 1990) and *The Good News according to Luke,* by Eduard Schweizer (Westminster Press, 1987). Check your church library for other resources.

Session 7:
How to Lead Discussions

Opening (10 minutes)

Write two headings on the chalkboard: "Strengths" and "Weaknesses." Invite the class to brainstorm about these questions: "What do you feel are the strengths of discussion as a teaching method?" "What are its weaknesses?" Ask them to respond in rapid-fire style, while you list their comments on the chalkboard.

Presentation (20 minutes)

Introduce the session in this way:
In today's session we will do three things:

1. Consider leadership styles that are most conducive to creating the atmosphere of openness and trust necessary for good discussion.
2. Learn how to ask good questions to facilitate discussion.
3. Explore different types of questions.

Leadership styles

In her book *Using the Bible in Groups,* Roberta Hestenes defines the four most common styles of group leadership, noting that some are more helpful than others. She identifies the four as:

1. Autocratic: domineering and dictatorial; more interested in subject matter than in people
2. Authoritative: definite yet responsive to the group; tries to involve others
3. Democratic: group-centered; leader and members share functions
4. Laissez-faire: permissive and passive; exercises minimal control

Hestenes has observed that in most new small groups, an authoritative leader (*not* an autocratic one) is more helpful in the beginning than one who leaves all decisions to inexperienced group members. Later, the group can move to a more democratic mode, with group members sharing as equal partners in decision making about procedures. The problem with autocratic leadership is that it can smother the ideas and opinions of group members. The problem with laissez-faire leadership is that discussions wander and the group accomplishes little.[4]

Ask the class, Can you give an example of a time when you experienced any of these four types of leadership? How did you feel as a member of the group? Continue the presentation:

Discussion questions

Asking good questions is an art. Discussion can be encouraged or stifled by the way in which questions are asked. Most of us have experienced the "Can you read my mind?" kind of question or intimidating ones that leave us feeling foolish and uncertain. Good discussion is based on respect for other persons and for their ideas and opinions. It is not one-upmanship. It involves a figurative sort of *leaning into* the other person through careful and attentive listening. It assumes that the leader does not have all the information and that class members' ideas are also significant.

The leader's role is to be aware of all group members, encouraging those who are hesitant and checking those who want to dominate. This takes both sensitivity and objectivity. Leaders can use encouraging phrases such as "Would you like to say more about that?" and give both verbal and nonverbal signs that they are listening intently. They can allow for silences, so that students feel they have the opportunity to talk. Above all, it is important for leaders to keep in mind that discussion is not a "time filler" but can be the heart and substance of learning.

Types of questions

Educator Don Griggs has given some helpful suggestions on the types of questions that facilitate discussion. He categorizes them in three ways: personal, analytical, and informational—or for brevity's sake, "P-A-I questions." Each type of question is used for a different purpose.

> P—*Personal level of questions:* Questions related to a person's own life experience. Their intent is to guide learners in personal decision making and value forming. For example: "If you had been the father of the prodigal son, what would you have done when he came home?"
>
> A—*Analytical level of questions:* Questions that require learners to think. These questions are open to many different answers or re-

sponses. They suggest that the teacher really wants to know what the learner thinks. For example: "What do you think the father in the prodigal son parable meant when he said, 'Son, you are always with me . . . '?"

    I—*Information level of questions.* Questions that require students to remember facts. It is almost impossible to have a good discussion guided by information questions. These must be followed up with analytical or personal questions. For example: "What did the younger son do with his share of the property?" has only one answer. To explore the parable further, the teacher must then ask another question, such as "How do you think that made him feel?"[5]

Exploration (20 minutes)

To improve skills in identifying and developing the three types of questions, ask students to do the following exercise:

1.   Open your Bibles to Luke 15:11–32.
2.   Classify the following questions according to the three types: (P) personal, (A) analytical, (I) informational. Then answer each question briefly.

> Who are the three main characters in the parable?
>
> Why do you think Jesus told this parable?
>
> If you had been the younger son, how would you have felt as you were walking back to your father?
>
> What feelings do you think the father had when the younger son left home? When he returned home? When the older son inquired about the party?
>
> What did the younger son say to himself when he decided to return to his father?
>
> What are some times when you have been forgiven by someone? How did you feel?
>
> What do you think this parable teaches us about the relationship between God and persons?

3.   Discuss your answers with one other person.[6]

Response (5 minutes)

Ask students to complete this sentence with a poetic image: "A good discussion is like. . . . " Ask two or three to share their sentences aloud.

Conclusion (5 minutes)

Close by reading this quote from *To Know as We Are Known*, by Parker Palmer:

Practicing responsive listening between teacher, students, and subject, is not finally a matter of technique. It depends ultimately on a teacher who has a living relationship with the subject at hand, who invites students into that relationship as full partners.[7]

Assignment for Next Time

Answer these questions in writing: "What is the most effective small-group Bible study you have experienced? What was the purpose of the group? What made it effective?"

Session 8:
Inductive Bible Study

Opening (10 minutes)

Ask students to share their homework assignments.

Presentation (20 minutes)

Introduce the topic in this way:

There are certain common threads in any good Bible study. You have identified some of them in your homework assignment. (Mention some of the points that the class raised in their homework.) Good Bible studies are discussions, not lectures, because the ultimate aim of Bible study is not the accumulation of knowledge but application of the scripture's teachings to our own lives. One approach to Bible study is called the inductive, or "discovery," method. Its purpose is to study scripture in a systematic way in three steps:

1. Observation: reading and reflecting on a scripture passage to ascertain the facts (using information questions)
2. Interpretation: trying to ascertain the author's purpose and the context (using analytical questions)
3. Application: determining the relevance of the passage for faith and life today (using personal questions)

The inductive or discovery method requires paying careful attention to the text before moving on to its application. It is a method for digging into the text without previous training and builds excitement as people make discoveries for themselves about the meaning of the Bible. While inductive study is demanding in terms of preparation and effort, many people prefer it because so much is learned in the process.

Inductive Bible study may take a number of forms: chapter study, book study, thematic or topical study (the popular Kerygma thematic Bible study is an example), word study, or biographical study.

The process for inductive study is this:

The leader prepares by selecting a passage of scripture, studying it carefully, and developing a set of questions geared toward factual information, analysis of what is happening, and personal application. Group members read the assigned passage. The group leader asks questions for discussion, using the three types: instructional, analytical and personal application. It helps to mention the verses where the answers can be found. After the first response, ask if anyone else has something to add. Begin with the instructional and analytical questions, but be sure to save enough time for personal application.[8]

Exploration (15 minutes)

Ask students to read Luke 15:11–32. Write these questions on the chalkboard, and ask students to find the answers:

1. Observation: What are the basic facts in this passage?
2. Interpretation: Why does the father run to meet the younger son?
3. Application: What does this passage say to you about the times when you feel "unworthy"?

Response (10 minutes)

Ask learners to create three new questions of observation, interpretation, and application about the parable.

Conclusion (5 minutes)

Ask learners to share some of the questions they have created with the class.

Assignment for Next Time

Ask learners to watch a movie or TV drama and write down lines of dialogue that have religious significance.

Session 9:
Using Drama to Teach

Opening (10 minutes)

Begin by asking learners to read the dialogue they have taken from movies or TV. Ask the class to identify what each line teaches about faith.

Then ask the students, Are there movies or TV series that are based entirely on religious topics? What kind of approach do they take toward religion—satirical, sympathetic, sentimental, realistic, or humorous?

Presentation (10 minutes)

Make the following introduction:

In medieval times, the church began to use drama as a way of traditioning and teaching people who were unable to read the Bible. It is still an effective way to teach biblical stories and provide encounters with the Christian faith, because it relates spiritual concepts to everyday life in nonthreatening terms. Drama also opens the door for further discussion and activities, because it summons up strong emotions and responses.

Many types of drama can be effective teaching tools in the church. These include play readings, role-plays, choral speaking, acting out biblical stories, dramatic reading of scripture, dialogue sermons, sermon monologues, involving the audience in dramatic reading, reader's theater, mime, writing dramatic scenes, musicals, and chancel dramas.

Some people may initially feel intimidated by drama, but you can begin to overcome their anxiety by using simple "warm-up" exercises. One easy exercise is to ask students to take turns repeating Luke 15:23, "This son of mine was dead and is alive again," but to say it with one of the following attitudes, which you will assign: disbelief, excitement, disgust, shock and fear, fury, wariness, joy.

Exploration (30 minutes)

Explain to the students that they are going to experience four forms of short drama that can be used in teaching or worship: dramatic reading of scripture, mime, the dramatic sermon, and role-playing.

1. *Dramatized reading of scripture* may be used in chancel worship as a way to bring alive narrative scripture texts. For a worship service, it is advisable to select readers ahead of time and ask them to rehearse the parts at least once together. A narrator

reads the parts of scripture that are not dialogue. Readers should put expression and feeling into their parts.

2. *Mime* is a classic theater form that uses no words, only gestures. A narrator may read the words while the cast acts out the story silently.

3. *Dramatic sermons* take a variety of forms. First-person sermons in which the preacher plays the role of the biblical person and sermons that re-create stories vividly are examples.

4. *Role-play* is an excellent dramatic tool for helping learners apply scripture to their own lives. In role-play, participants try to act out the feelings of people in a hypothetical situation. For role-play to be successful, the teacher must establish a climate in which learners feel safe, knowing that their efforts will be appreciated and that they will not be put down for their interpretations. One way to introduce the technique is to select several persons beforehand and go over the material with them so that they will feel more at ease. However, it is important that after this first introductory time, the exercise be spontaneous. Always follow the role-play with discussion, asking questions that help learners understand the scene and apply it to their lives.

Divide the class into four groups. Each group will have seven minutes to carry out the following instructions:

Group One: Provide a dramatized reading of the parable in Luke 15:11–32. Select members of the group to read the dialogue ascribed to the younger brother, the father, the elder son, and the slave. Select another group member to be the narrator, reading all the nondialogue verses.

Group Two: Mime the passage while it is being read aloud. Select a narrator to do the reading, and assign parts to the rest of the group.

Group Three: Present a dramatic sermon. Choose someone from your group to read "The Prodigal Son," by James Weldon Johnson, with great fervor.

Group Four: Select two members of the group to role-play a conversation between the two brothers in the parable of the prodigal son who find themselves sitting next to each other at the "Welcome Home" banquet. Select a group member to ask this question of the players after the role-play: "What was going on inside you when you played the older/younger brother?"

Response (5 minutes)

Ask each student to share which dramatic form he or she found most effective and to explain why.

Conclusion (5 minutes)

Ask one of the students to close with prayer.

Assignment for Next Time

Answer this question: "What is a learning center?" Describe any experience you may have had with learning centers, as a teacher or as a student.

Session 10:
Learning Centers for All Ages

Preparation

Print the following Chinese proverb on a piece of poster board:

> I hear and I forget.
> I see, and I remember.
> I do and I understand.
> —Chinese proverb.

Prepare instructions in the "Exploration" section for the three learning centers, worksheets (Appendix, page 132), and information sheets (pages 133–35).

Gather from your church library or denominational resource center several books of creative activities.

Make a copy for each student of Proverbs 3:5–8.

Opening (5 minutes)

Draw the students' attention to the Chinese proverb, which you have displayed on the bulletin board or wall, and ask, What are the implications of this proverb for teaching? Allow time for the class to respond.

Presentation (15 minutes)

Deliver the following information:

What are learning centers? If you have ever visited a preschool classroom, you know the answer. Learning centers are simply areas set aside for individualized learning. They offer opportunities for students to explore subject matter through special activities such as research, creative writing, art, music, and response to pictures. Individualized learning allows people not only to use their special skills and explore special interests but to proceed at their own speed. Learning centers are widely accepted in young children's classes, but they can also be exciting for youth and adults.

In addition to the educational benefits derived from learning centers, I believe there are four theological reasons that learning centers should be used:

1. God made each person a unique individual, with different learning abilities and interest levels from everyone else. Good teaching recognizes and honors those differences by finding ways for individual expression and different learning skills.
2. God created us with the ability to make choices. The best learning method is one that allows choices and helps persons learn to choose appropriately.
3. God's covenant with us demands that we learn to accept responsibility. The learning center approach is consistent with this, because it gives each learner an opportunity to share responsibility for his or her own learning.
4. God created us to live in relationship with God and others. The learning center atmosphere promotes relationships as learners work with each other and with the teacher.

The procedure for using learning centers in a class is as follows:

1. The teacher sets up the centers in the classroom beforehand, making each center as attractive as possible, and provides instructions and all the materials needed to carry out those instructions.
2. The teacher opens the class by presenting the topic or theme. The presentation may take the form of a brief video, a lecture, a presentation by a guest speaker, or another introductory method.
3. The students go to the center of their choice for further exploration of the theme. The centers should offer some of the following: Bible research; artwork; creative writing; response to

pictures, symbols, or music; and games or puzzles. The activities in the center should be appropriate to the ages and abilities of the students.

4. After spending time in one or more centers, learners reconvene to share what they have done.

Exploration (20 minutes)

Explain to students that they will learn more about learning centers by actually experiencing how they work.

Invite students to spend 5 minutes or so in each of the following learning centers:

Center 1. Facts about Learning Centers

On the table for this center, place copies of the information sheets, pencils, a copy of the worksheet for each student, and the following instructions:

Skim the information sheets and fill out the worksheets. Take your worksheet with you when you have finished, but leave the information sheets on the table.

Center 2. Choosing Learning Activities

Place on the table the resource books you have gathered, blank paper, pencils, and a card with these instructions:

Using the resource books on the table, identify and write down three activities that help express the meaning of the parable of the prodigal son. Specify the age group for which the activities would be appropriate. Note the book in which the idea was found, for future reference.

Center 3. Creating a Center

Place on the table a card with these instructions:

Choose one of the activities you discovered in Center 2, and write a plan for a learning center based on that activity. Identify the purpose and the materials necessary, and supply instructions for the learners.

Response (5 minutes)

Gather the class together to share what they learned about centers through today's experience.

Conclusion (5 minutes)

Hand out to each student a copy of Proverbs 3:5–8, and ask students to read the verses together.

Assignment for Next Time

Ask class members to complete the sentence "Poetry is . . ."

Session 11:
Creative Writing

Preparation

Prepare a poster with this quote:

We do not write in order to be understood: we write in order to understand.

—C. Day Lewis

Tape the poster to the wall.

For Center 1: Tape a four-foot length of plain shelf paper to the wall. Provide colored felt-tip markers.

For Center 2: Supply paper, pencils, construction paper, glue.

For Center 3: Provide paper and pencils.

For Center 4: Provide bumper-sticker-size strips of paper and markers.

For Center 5: Provide paper and pencils.

For all centers: Prepare instruction cards as described for each center in the "Exploration" section below.

Opening (10 minutes)

Ask volunteers in the class to read aloud their homework poems.

Presentation (10 minutes)

Introduce the topic this way:

Creative writing not only allows people to give expression to their faith experience; as C. Day Lewis reminds us, it helps them understand it and, in the process of articulation, move forward in their faith journey. It is also a wonderful way of "traditioning," for as people become better able to describe their own faith, they become more capable of passing on what is truly important about it.

Ask learners to share their sentence completions about poetry. What do they reveal about the learners' attitudes toward creative writing? Acknowledge that many persons have negative feelings about imaginative or creative writing, especially poetry. Suggest that teachers can help dispel these feelings by stressing that writing is just conversation written down; by using writing exercises that are fun, not tedious; by affirming learners' efforts; by giving up the temptation to correct spelling and punctuation; and by encouraging learners to forget rhyming and to put their emphasis on creating vivid images.

Exploring (25 minutes)

Use the learning center approach. Set up centers on tables in the classroom and provide instructions and all necessary materials.

Center 1. Creating Graffiti

Instructions:

How do you think the younger son in Luke 15:11–32 felt when his father kissed him? Express those feelings in graffiti on the sheet of paper on the wall.

Center 2. Writing a Poem

Instructions:

Write a poem based on the parable of the prodigal son. Glue your poem to a sheet of construction paper and leave it on the table.

Center 3. Writing a Letter

Instructions:

Imagine you were one of the neighbors present at the return of the younger brother. Write a letter to a friend, describing what you saw and how you felt.

Center 4. Create a Bumper Sticker

Instructions:

On a strip of paper, create a bumper-sticker slogan suggested by the parable of the prodigal son.

Center 5. The Rest of the Story

Instructions:

What do you think happened after the father's speech to the older brother? Write the rest of the story as you think it might have occurred.

Response (10 minutes)

Leave enough time to assemble the class. Ask the students, What new insight did you gain into the parable through these writing exercises?

Conclusion (5 minutes)

Ask for a volunteer to share his or her poem about the parable with the class.

Assignment for Next Time

Bring to class a religious art print that you like.

Session 12:
Teaching with Art

Preparation

For Center 1: Provide a supply of magazines, large sheets of construction paper, scissors, and glue.

For Center 2: Provide potter's clay or self-hardening clay, toothpicks (for making details), fine wire (for cutting the clay), squares of wax paper (to set the clay on).

For Center 3: Provide shelf paper or finger-paint paper, water, and finger paints. (Finger paints can be made by sprinkling powdered tempera paint on liquid starch and mixing with a brush.)

For Center 4: Make a copy of the tangram design (see Appendix, page 136) for each student. It should be about three and a half square inches to fit on a nine-by-twelve-inch sheet of background paper. Cut the pieces apart and place each tangram in an envelope. Supply construction paper for background.

For Center 5: Display as many pictures as you can find of the prodigal son. Some good sources are Henri Nouwen's *The Return of the Prodigal Son* (New York: Doubleday, 1992), Bruce Barnard's *The Bible and Its Pictures* (New York: Macmillan Publishing Co., 1983), and anthologies of religious art. Provide watercolors, charcoal, pastels, soft lead pencils, and sketch paper.

Make instruction cards for all centers, as described in the "Exploration" section below.

Arrange a way to display artwork: on a bulletin board; on a string hung across a corner of the room, with paper clips to attach pictures; by taping to the walls.

Opening (10 minutes)

Begin the class by asking learners to share their pictures with the class. Have them explain why they selected the picture.

Presentation (10 minutes)

Make a brief presentation of the following information:

A recent study has shown that in our society, over 90 percent of the population measures "high creativity" at age five. By age seven, (second grade), that number drops to 10 percent, and by adulthood, to 2 percent! This repression of creativity is surely one of the greatest tragedies of growing up. Sometimes it takes people a lifetime to discover the creativity that has been buried deep within them. We are all more creative than we imagine, but we need help in drawing out that creativity, in being emboldened to express it, and in learning to combat those inner voices that whisper in our ears, "Yours isn't any good; you can't do it." We have a twofold responsibility in teaching: to develop our own creativity and to encourage the creativity of our students.

Teachers need not be artists to make art an important part of the teaching experience. Your role is to be a catalyst: to structure opportunities for creativity according to the time and space, the raw materials, and the encouragement your students will need. To encourage creativity, teachers must learn how to greet unusual ideas and questions with respect and interest, so that learners will feel their ideas have value.

There are four requirements of art activities. They must be:

1. Purposeful: Art activities should enable learners to experience something in a new, fresh way.
2. Proportionate: Art activities should fit the time available.
3. Personal: Art activities should satisfy, reward, fulfill, and challenge.
4. Penetrating: Art activities must draw learners into new depths of perception.

Exploration (25 minutes)

Since the best way to learn is by firsthand experience, use the learning center approach in your class. Set up the following five centers on different tables. Ask learners to participate in as many centers as time allows.

Center 1. Picture Collage

Instructions:

Select pictures from magazines that express to you the meaning of the story of the prodigal son. Glue them on the construction paper background, overlapping them in collage style.

Center 2. Clay and Sculpture Center

Instructions:

Work with the clay, softening it and molding it to create a shape that symbolizes the forgiveness expressed by the father in the parable.

Center 3. Finger-Paint Center

Instructions:

Place several tablespoons of paint on damp paper and move it around with fingers, hands, or even arms. Try to express the feelings of the younger son when his father put his arms around him and kissed him, or the feelings of the older son when he came home and learned what was going on. Label your work, and spread it on a table to dry.

Center 4. Tangram Center

Instructions:

A tangram is a square that has been cut into seven pieces. These pieces can be arranged to form many designs. The designs can be realistic or symbolic.

Take the pieces of paper in the envelope and glue them to a sheet of paper in a way that represents to you a scene from the prodigal son story.

Center 5. Drawing or Painting

Instructions:

Study the artists' interpretations of the parable. Then, draw or paint your own version.

Response (10 minutes)

Provide an opportunity for everyone to view the artworks made by class members. Display art on tables, taped to walls, hung by paper clips from a string stretched across a corner, or thumbtacked to bulletin boards.

Conclusion (5 minutes)

Close with a prayer of gratitude for the joy of creativity and for the artists who have enriched our faith understanding.

Assignment for Next Time

Final exam! Create a learning center for adults based on a biblical story or theological concept that took on fresh meaning for you in the two previous segments of the teacher training course ("Basic Biblical Background" and "Foundations for Faith"). Bring to class all the materials you will need for the center and an attractive instruction card. On a sheet of paper, write the theme, the purpose of the center, a list of materials needed, and the list of instructions. Make copies of this sheet for each member of the class. Be prepared to set the center up in class and explain your concept.

Session 13:
Summary Session

Preparation

Arrange tables around the room.

Make copies of the evaluation sheet (see Appendix, page 137) for all class members.

Opening (10 minutes)

As people arrive, ask them to set up their centers on the tables you have placed around the room.

Presentation (30 minutes)

Ask learners to take turns presenting their centers and distributing handouts to other students.

Exploration (5 minutes)

When everyone has finished, convene the whole class. Ask for reactions to the process of designing a center. Were there problems or difficulties? Was it difficult to select an appropriate activity? Do you feel that adults will respond enthusiastically to your center? Do you think it is something you will use in the future?

Response (10 minutes)

In this section, class members will respond to the entire program. Ask learners to complete the evaluation sheet of the three courses. (See Appendix, page 137.)

Conclusion (5 minutes)

Read to the class Ephesians 4:11–16, and close with prayer.

Equipping the Saints

The word that is translated in Ephesians 4:12 as "equip" is a Greek medical term that literally means "set a bone." This verse in Ephesians is the only time Paul uses the term, and the implications are fascinating. If the "saints" are to be equipped for the work of ministry, they need to be able to "walk the walk," not just "talk the talk." They must be not crippled in their understanding of faith but strong and vigorous for the tasks to which they have been called.

The process of setting bones is not accomplished overnight. It requires the help of skilled persons, who use their knowledge to make sure the bones are properly aligned for the best results. It usually requires the support of a cast during the time in which the bone is growing into firmness and solidity. It may also be necessary to depend on other persons for their support and caring while one is incapacitated. Knowing what to expect and feeling that progress is being made greatly boosts one's morale. And, finally, there is tremendous joy when the cast is off and the doctor pronounces the bone "ready for action."

For of all these reasons, bone setting is an apt metaphor for equipping teachers. In this chapter, we explore some of its implications.

THE HELP OF SKILLED PERSONS

The preceding chapters have laid out a plan to train persons for the task of traditioning the faith. Clearly, the persons responsible for teaching the three segments must be skilled teachers themselves. They must have a knowledge of the Bible and the basic beliefs of the Christian tradition and also an understanding of the principles of good teaching and learning. This must not be a case of "the blind leading the blind" but of providing the best possible expertise.

A SUPPORTIVE FRAMEWORK: "THE CAST"

It would be ridiculous for a doctor to set the broken wrist of a ball player and send him immediately back into the game with the instructions: "Now get out there and pitch!" Unfortunately, this is what happens all too often in the church. Even when persons have had opportunities to learn from skilled teachers, and even when those teachers have done an excellent job of "bone-setting," the trainees are seldom ready to "get out there and pitch."

The best method of learning how to teach a given age group is what could be called the "cast method." Instead of launching out all alone, the new teacher learns by observing an expert and then teaching under guidance. The process provides support, just as a cast supports the bone while it grows.

Lab Schools

In the 1960s and early '70s, there was a great emphasis on "lab schools." These were usually planned by denominations or ecumenical groups, so that prospective teachers from many churches could attend. The very best possible teachers were asked to teach a representative age group in order to demonstrate skilled teaching. These lab schools were extremely helpful in developing teachers, because new teachers could see firsthand how to use varied methods, respond to learners' questions, and handle discipline problems.

Lab schools have almost disappeared, but their place has been taken by an expanding list of excellent videotapes that demonstrate teaching of different age levels, such as the Presbyterian Learning and Leading video series, available from Presbyterian Distribution Service, 100 Witherspoon St., Louisville, KY 40202-1396.

Visitations

Another method in developing your new teaching skills is to visit a class in one's own church or to make arrangements to visit another church in order to see a teacher of a certain age group in action. It is extremely important that you get the teacher's permission first. Many teachers find it very difficult to teach with another person observing, so the observer must make sure that the teacher has no objections. Observation should be done as unobtrusively as possible, without calling attention to oneself through comments or asides. It is a good idea to take notes, especially of how the session is developed. Note the following:

How does the room setting help with the learning process?

What does the teacher do when the first learners arrive?
What happens in the five parts of the lesson (opening, presenting,
    exploring, responding, concluding)?
How is the Bible used?

A SUPPORTIVE NETWORK
OF PERSONS WHO CARE

Apprenticeship

Even better than observing from the sidelines is a process that allows for guidance and feedback. Apprenticeship has long been used as an effective way to learn a skill. In fact, before the advent of vocational training in schools, it was the only way to learn a trade.

Apprenticeship has four stages. The first is observation: watching, noticing, learning by seeing. The second is assisting: assuming minor responsibilities at first, then graduating to more difficult tasks. The third is teaching the class under the watchful eye of the teacher, who can then provide a friendly evaluation of your performance. The fourth stage is teaching alone, without a mentor present.

Tutorials

A very helpful idea for the ongoing support of a new teacher is a once-a-week, face-to-face conversation with a more experienced teacher. The latter may be the minister, the church educator, or another classroom teacher. The tutorial gives the learner an opportunity to talk about how the class went, reporting actual happenings and conversations. In addition, the next week's session can be previewed, and the more experienced teacher can make suggestions about methods, resources, and so forth. A tutorial is a wonderful opportunity for a minister to play the role of "teacher of teachers."

Opportunities for Further Training

Even when a teacher has completed the basic course outlined in this book, it is important that he or she continue to pursue other training opportunities. Most denominations have regional schools or teacher workshops that offer a variety of courses for teachers. These are especially supportive in the help they provide with methods and resources for particular age groups.

Libraries and Resource Centers

Many churches and denominational offices have libraries and resource centers, providing the latest books and videos for improving your teaching and supplementing curriculum. Become a serious reader of books on teaching methods, lesson planning, Bible study, and so forth that are available in these centers.

Exchange of Ideas

Perhaps the best support a new teacher can possibly have is other teachers. Informal conversation about resources, methods, discipline techniques, and training opportunities can be invaluable. Sharing joys and successes can help build enthusiasm and optimism.

Praise and Affirmation

Affirmation and recognition of teachers' work gives them support, encouragement, and a sense of worth and achievement. One way to accomplish this is by reporting unusual class projects or studies in the church newsletter or on a bulletin board. Appreciation dinners can also be effective ways of recognizing and affirming teachers.

It is impossible to overestimate the importance of the pastor's role in affirmation, recognition, and support. When a pastor shows personal interest in what the teacher is doing, offers praise and encouragement, and calls attention to good teaching both in sermons and in conversation with others, this support carries enormous weight. Even when a church has a professional church educator, the pastor's affirmation is extremely important. If the pastor recognizes the call of those who are called to the task of traditioning and affirms it as genuine ministry, then the eyes of the whole church can be opened to the importance of this task.

Concrete Rewards

A church I am familiar with was concerned about the low regard in which Sunday school teachers were held. It decided to begin paying its teachers a small honorarium and charging a small tuition fee to all learners. If teachers were reluctant to accept the honorarium, they were invited to use it to purchase extra teaching materials for their class (books, maps, art supplies, etc.). The result was a tremendous boost in morale. Teachers felt as if the church valued their gifts and talents. Most did recycle their honoraria into resources, but that did not diminish their feeling that the church appreciated them.

I realize that payment of church teachers is a sensitive issue, but I have long wondered why we are so willing to pay organists, soloists, sextons, supply preachers, professional educators, and ministers and so unwilling to pay those who teach every Sunday in the church's classrooms. Is it because these teachers lack the professional qualifications and training possessed by those in the other categories? Are training and professionalism what we reward financially? If this is the case, then teachers who have been through the nine-month teacher training proposed in this book surely deserve some financial evidence of recognition and respect.

There is a more important reason, however, to affirm concretely those who teach in the church. It is the acknowledgment that they are called by God for the work of ministry, "for building up the body of Christ," just as much as those who are ordained to the ministry of Word and sacrament. If we truly believe this, then we must use every means possible to communicate to church teachers that we recognize, affirm, and rejoice in their call and are grateful for their service.

KNOWING WHAT TO EXPECT

In his book *Effective Church Leadership*, Harris Lee has summarized what people need in order to do their best:

> to know what will be expected of them;
> to have a sense of belonging and that they are wanted;
> to have responsibilities that challenge and yet are within range of their abilities;
> to have confidence in the leadership of the group.[1]

All too often, we neglect these important criteria in calling people into God's service. We ask them to "teach the junior highs," without specifying whether they are making a commitment for three months, three years, or a lifetime. We give them very little information about the students they will be teaching, the classroom setting, or the curriculum resources with which they will be provided. We do not do a good job of affirming that they are wanted and valued. To make matters worse, many times these teachers feel overwhelmed by the difficulties of the task they have undertaken, yet they do not receive much help in handling these difficulties. All these factors can certainly undermine the confidence volunteers have in the leader who issued the call, whether it be a committee, a board, the director of Christian education, or the pastor.

Equipping the Saints

One of the best ways to help teachers know what to expect is by having written job descriptions. A job description enables a prospective teacher to make an informed decision about the task that he or she is being invited to consider. Such descriptions provide useful guides for functioning and help eliminate organizational confusion about who does what. They are also useful in evaluating performance.

Once a person has made a decision, it is extremely important to provide a written contract or covenant of agreement between the church and the teacher. Here are samples of a contract and a covenant that may be provided to the teacher.[2]

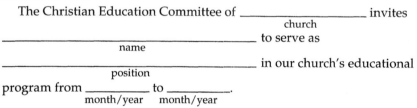

Mutual Agreement of Service

You are invited

The Christian Education Committee of _____ invites
church

_____ to serve as
name

_____ in our church's educational
position

program from _____ to _____.
month/year   month/year

A Covenant between Church and Teacher

Moved by love for God and the desire to do God's will and share God's love with others, I accept this teaching responsibility and pledge to my church and to God to:

1. Seek spiritual growth through Bible study and prayer as well as through regular congregational worship.
2. Grow in understanding my students, so that I may aid them in their growth as Christians.
3. Study and prepare thoroughly for every teaching session.
4. Participate in opportunities for in-service training.

Signed _____
Teacher

As fellow workers for God, we pledge to:

1. Support each teacher with prayer as we seek to do God's will together.
2. Provide the best possible teaching materials, equipment, and space.
3. Develop training opportunities to keep teachers alert and growing.
4. Plan opportunities for evaluation so that we may increase the effectiveness of our witness for Christ.

Signed _____
Minister

Signed _____
Chair, Christian
Education Committee

Note that the contract and covenant make clear the length of time of service, the expectations of the teacher, and the commitment of the pastor and Christian education committee or governing body. In this way, teachers do not feel they are signing on for a lifetime. The contract can be renewed if both parties of the covenant feel it is appropriate in the light of God's call.

FEELING THAT PROGRESS HAS BEEN MADE

I have filled out hundreds of evaluation forms of conferences, events, persons, even sermons, and I will not pretend it is my favorite sport. And yet, in my years of planning continuing education events for a seminary, I became aware of how vitally important evaluations are. They are the "finger on the pulse" of learning events where there are no tests and grades. It was through those evaluations that I was able to discern if an event had worked well and had met the expectations of the students who participated in it.

Individual Questionnaires

Evaluation can be an extremely powerful tool for growth. Teachers need to look at their own performances and also need evaluations from their students. An individual questionnaire does not have to be a complex form but can consist of a few thoughtful questions at the end of the term of service.

A personal evaluation could include such questions as:

> What seemed to work well?
> What did your students seem to enjoy most?
> What seemed most to help? to hinder?
> How well do you feel you achieved your personal objectives?
> How eager are you to teach again?

Students could be asked to answer these questions during the last class:

> What did you like best about this year (or semester, quarter, etc.)
> What did you like least about this year?
> What would you suggest to make next year's classes better?[3]

Formal Meetings

It is very helpful for the entire teaching and leadership staff to meet at the end of the year in order to discuss what went well and to make suggestions for the next year. This meeting can serve as a "pep talk" to create excitement and a sense of achievement and accomplishment. It should not be allowed to degenerate into a complaint session.

Informal Sessions

Instead of a formal meeting at the end of the year, many churches hold a potluck supper for teachers, with informal discussion about how things are going. This meeting could also include an inspirational note, with singing and prayers for each teacher.

Personal Interviews

Perhaps the best way of evaluating teacher performance is to take the time for a personal conversation. This type of conversation creates an environment for honest sharing of feelings and can provide valuable feedback. Normally, the interview is conducted by the director of Christian education or the minister, but it could also be led by the Sunday school superintendent or chair of the Christian education committee. Such interviews prevent teachers from feeling that they have been left to "sink or swim" and reassure them that someone cares about them and their work.

READY FOR ACTION

The bones are set; it's time to run the race! But before teachers begin their service, one more important step remains.

A service of consecration and public recognition at the beginning of a term of service is the church's acknowledgment of a person's sense of call. The service should be held during regular congregational worship, so that the entire congregation can take part in affirming that call. A possible order for such a service follows.[4]

Service of Consecration of Teachers
1. Introduction of the whole teaching staff
2. Charge to the staff by the minister
3. Pledge by the staff:
   Relying on God for guidance and help, we accept this trust and dedicate ourselves to these tasks of teaching and leadership. We will give ourselves gladly and sincerely to this work of the church family, doing our best to live, to study, and to exemplify the life of a disciple of the Great Teacher.
4. Charge to the congregation by the minister

5. Pledge by the congregation:

    We, the people of this church, pledge our active participation in and support of the educational work of the church, seeking always to continue our own learning and growth as Christians. We will pray with and for the church's teachers and leaders. We will strive by personal example to testify to our love for Christ and his kingdom, God being our helper.

6. Prayer of dedication by the minister:

O God,
For calling these teachers into ministry,
   We give thanks.
For their willingness to answer that call,
   We give thanks.
For the gifts they bring and the commitment they offer,
   We give thanks.
For their dedication over the past months to this time of preparation,
   We give thanks.
In joy and gratitude, we dedicate these servants
   To the work of your kingdom.
In the name of the Master Teacher, Jesus Christ, Amen.

At the end of this service, the covenants signed by the teachers, the minister, and the chair of the Christian education committee may be reverently placed in the offering plates, as a concrete symbol of the act of dedication.

THE CAUTION

There it is, in the epistle of James: "Not many of you should become teachers, my brothers and sisters, for you know that we who teach will be judged with greater strictness" (James 3:1). What a scary thought!

At no other place in scripture is the tremendous responsibility of traditioning the faith taken more seriously. James's caution is a call to a faithful embodiment of the faith that is being taught, so that teachers' "lips and lives" will make a joint confession of obedience to God.

And yet James goes on to say, "For all of us make many mistakes" (3:2). Teaching in the church will never be perfect, any more than the teachers' lives will be flawless. But the church's responsibility is to start putting the horse before the cart: doing everything in its power for those who are called to the task of traditioning the faith, so that their teaching will be accurate, faithful, discerning, compassionate, and inspired, to the end that "everyone who belongs to God may be proficient, equipped for every good work" (2 Tim. 3:17).

Appendix

Supplemental Handout

WORKSHEET

Gen. 1:1–2:3	Questions to Answer	Gen. 2:4–25
1.	How long did creation take?	1.
2.	Where did creation take place?	2.
3.	When in the process was man created?	3.
4.	When in the process was woman created?	4.
5.	From what substance are man and woman created?	5.
6.	What is the relationship between male and female?	6.
7.	What is the relationship between human beings and God?	7.
8.	What is the main point, idea, or message of the story?	8.

122

Supplemental Handout

RULERS OF THE DIVIDED KINGDOM

	Judah	*Israel*
922 B.C.	Rehoboam (7 years)	Jeroboam I (22 years)
	Abijah/Abijam (3 months)	
	Asa (41 years)	Nadab (2 years)
		Baasha (24 years)
		Elah (2 years)
		Zimri, Tibni (7 days)
		Omri (12 years)
	Jehoshaphat (25 years)	
874 B.C.		Ahab (22 years)
		Ahaziah (2 years)
	Jehoram/Joram (8 years)	
		Jehoram (12 years)
	Ahaziah (6 years)	Jehu (28 years)
	Athaliah (6 years)	
	*Joash/Jehoash (40 years)	
		Jehoahaz (17 years)
	Amaziah (29 years)	
		Jeroboam II (41 years)
783 B.C.	Azariah/Uzziah (52 years)	
	Jotham (16 years)	
		Zechariah (6 months)
		Shallum (1 month)
		Menahem (10 years)
		Pekahiah (2 years)
		Pekah (20 years)
735 B.C.	Ahaz (16 years)	Hoshea (9 years)
	*Hezekiah (29 years)	
	Manasseh (55 years)	
	Amon (2 years)	
640 B.C.	*Josiah (31 years)	
	Jehoahaz (3 months)	
	Jehoiakim (11 years)	
598 B.C.	Jehoiachin (3 months)	
596 B.C.	Zedekiah (11 years)	

---

*The "good" kings.

Supplemental Handout

THE GOSPELS

Gospel:

> The word *gospel* in Greek literally means "good news."
> The four Gospels are writings that announce the good news of God's entry into history in Jesus.

Synoptic Gospels:

> Matthew, Mark, and Luke are called the Synoptic Gospels because they describe the events of Jesus' life in much the same way.
> The word *synoptic* in Greek means "seeing together" or "coming from the same perspective."
> John's Gospel is not considered a Synoptic Gospel, because his perspective is different from that of the other Gospel writers. He goes beyond them in interpreting theologically the events of Jesus' life.

Matthew:

> Written for Christians of Jewish background between 80–100 A.D.
> Emphasizes the fulfillment of Old Testament prophecies to show that Jesus is indeed the Messiah, an authentic Jew and authentic king
> Emphasizes true righteousness as a characteristic of the kingdom of God

Mark:

> Considered the earliest of the Gospels, written for Christians of Gentile background before 70 A.D.
> Characterized by a sense of urgency and mystery
> Presents Jesus as "the wonder-working Servant of God"
> Wants to encourage Christians to believe in Jesus' power to deliver them from danger and to prepare for the coming kingdom

Luke:

> Written for Christians of a Greek background between 80–90 A.D.
> Stresses the compassion and tenderness of Jesus
> Has been called "the Gospel of the poor and lowly"

Supplemental Handout

John:

       More theological than the other three

       More interested in the symbolism underlying a story than in the story itself

       Uses symbols drawn from daily experience: bread, water, light, life, word, shepherd, door, way

       Records seven miracles, which the author refers to as signs that can evoke faith

WORKSHEET

**THE LAST SUPPER
ACCORDING TO THE GOSPEL WRITERS**

As you study and review the Gospel versions of the Last Supper, answer these questions:

What is the biggest difference in the way John describes the supper and the way the Synoptic Gospels describe it? What does John see as the most significant thing that happened at the supper? What is most significant for the Synoptics?

Which Gospel shows the most interest in Judas? Which shows the least?

What is the difference in the Gospels' versions of the disciples' response to Jesus declaring that he would be betrayed?

Which Gospel's wording is most often used in observing Communion in your church?

Which versions are most alike?

Supplemental Handout

SYMBOLS IN APOCALYPTIC LITERATURE

1. Numbers

7 = Perfection, completeness

3 = Heaven

4 = Earth

6 = Humankind

10 = Human completeness

12 = The church (heir of the 12 tribes)

3 1/2 = Incompleteness or suffering

144,000 = The total of all God's people (12 × 12 × 1,000)

666 = Falling short of completeness (7)

2. Colors

White = Righteousness, victory

Red = War

Black = Famine

Pale or ashen = Death

3. Specific Symbols in Revelation

Babylon = Rome

Book with seven seals = God's will

Seven trumpets = Warnings of judgment

Seven plagues or bowls = Judgment on Babylon

Seven candlesticks = The seven churches

Seven horns, seven eyes = All-powerful, all-seeing

Seven spirits = The Holy Spirit

The woman = God's people

The dragon = The forces of evil or Satan

The beasts = Rome and emperor worship

The elders = All faithful people

The lion = The triumphant Christ

The lamb = The suffering Christ

Sodom and Egypt = Evil and oppression

Supplemental Handout

WORKSHEET

TWO KINDS OF REVELATION

Read the following passages, which express general revelation. Write down the key idea about how God is revealed, as it appears in each passage.

Psalm 19
Acts 14:16–18
Acts 17:22–31
Romans 1:18–23
Romans 2:12–16

Now read these passages, which express special revelation. Write down the key idea about how God is revealed, as it appears in each passage.

John 1:1–14
John 14:9
2 Timothy 3:16–17
Ephesians 1:16–23
Colossians 1:15–20

Supplemental Handout

THE TRINITY

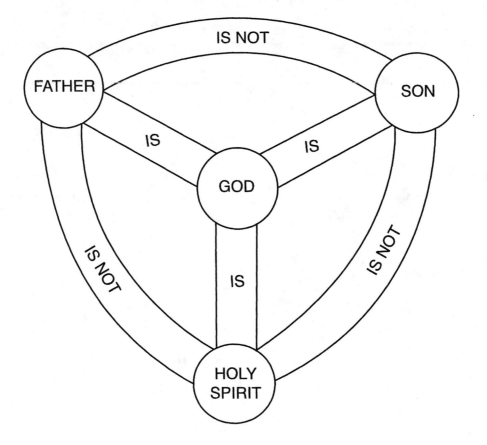

AGE-APPROPRIATE LEARNING ACTIVITIES

Nursery (2–3)

Drawing and painting with large crayons and wide brushes
Conversation
Learning simple stories and songs about Jesus
Playing with others
Wonderment at nature objects
Musical games

Preschool (4–6)

Singing, moving to music
Active movement games
Stories about Jesus and families
Drawing, painting, finger painting, clay
Conversation

Elementary (7–11)

Hearing and acting out Bible stories
Singing and illustrating hymns
Writing poems, prayers, litanies
Puzzles, crosswords, games
Drawing, painting
Memorizing Bible verses, Lord's Prayer

Early adolescence (12–14)

Bible study
Poetry, drama, art, and music
Lecture and discussion
Field trips
Time lines

Youth (15–18)

Brainstorming
Small-group discussions
Videos, pictures, maps
Directed reading

Supplemental Handout

Hands-on activities: field trips, work camps
Drama and role-play
Artwork

Young adults (19–30)

Lecture and discussion
Brainstorming
Inductive Bible study
Small-group discussion
Field trips and work camps
Artwork
Role-play and drama
Resource persons
Videos, films, pictures

Middle adults (31–55)

Lecture and discussion
Book reports
Interviewing a guest
Research and report
Small-group discussion
Videos, films, pictures
Brainstorming
Role-play
Inductive Bible study
Artwork

Older adults (55 and over)

Lecture and discussion
Small groups
Resource persons
Inductive Bible study
Videos, film, pictures

GUIDELINES FOR PREPARING TO TEACH

1. Read through the entire unit before beginning the first lesson, so that you understand its purpose and intent. Do additional reading and preparation as necessary.

2. Read through the session you will teach several days in advance (preferably a week), so that you will have time to look for illustrations of your subject in current events and life happenings.

3. Tailor the curriculum to fit your class. For instance, you may not have time to do all the exercises suggested. Choose those that are most appropriate for the persons in your class.

4. Make sure you have clearly in mind the "bottom line," or key concept, of the session you are about to lead. What message do your students need to take with them?

5. Plan specific methods or strategies to teach a lesson: opening, presenting, exploring, responding, and concluding.

6. Pray, study, and *think*.

Supplemental Handout

WORKSHEET

Directions: Read the information sheets to answer the following questions:

1. List two suggestions about room arrangements for learning centers.

2. What are two types of learning centers?

3. What are two tasks of the learning center leader?

INFORMATION SHEET 1

ROOM ARRANGEMENTS FOR LEARNING CENTERS

1. Set centers up on separate tables that will allow four or five persons to share the work space comfortably. Provide all necessary supplies and an instruction card (preferably laminated).

2. Use folding screens to separate a center from the rest of the class. Instructions can be taped to the screen and the finished work displayed on it. Learners can sit on cushions or on rugs on the floor in front of the screen.

3. Use large, refrigerator-type boxes as special storytelling or video centers. (This works especially well for children.)

4. Hang instruction cards from the ceiling or tack them to a bulletin board.

5. Make the center as attractive as possible. Use pictures to illustrate the theme. Display the work materials so that they look inviting; do not just pile them or stack them carelessly.

Supplemental Handout

INFORMATION SHEET 2

TYPES OF LEARNING CENTERS

Learning centers can take many different forms. Here are some of the alternatives:

1. Topical centers: Here, each center explores a different aspect of the theme. One center might present the geographical setting of a biblical story, another the historical context, while still another analyzes the people in the story. If the theme is "Creation," for example, six centers might be offered, one for each day of creation. Learners choose the centers as they wish.

2. Activity centers: The centers interpret the same theme through different activities, such as art, music, research, writing, drama, storytelling, and inductive study. Again, learners choose the centers.

3. Progressive centers: These are topical centers, but a learner participates in all the centers, rotating from one to another after a designated amount of time. This approach is generally extended over several sessions to allow all learners time to explore each center.

4. Required work centers: These can be either topical or activity centers, but they are not optional, and all learners are expected to complete two centers (Bible Study and Research) before they work in the other centers of their choice. This ensures that the learners are receiving specific content.

INFORMATION SHEET 3

TASKS OF THE LEARNING CENTER LEADER

Provide an environment that facilitates learning

Help orient the group to the process

Clarify directions

Encourage and assist participants

Exhibit sensitivity to the needs of each person

Guide learners as needed in making choices, locating resources, keeping to the task, and achieving appropriately

Serve as a resource person

Become involved in learning with the participants

Bring the group together for sharing and worship

Supplemental Handout

TANGRAM

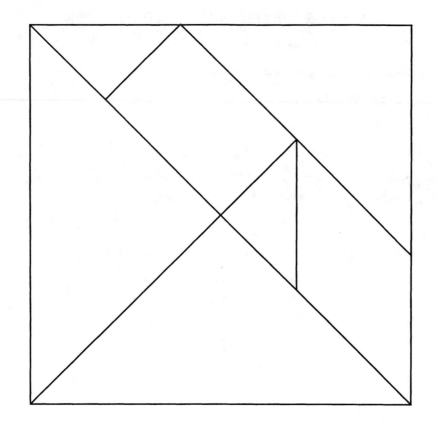

EVALUATION SHEET

Basic Biblical Background

What was the best thing about the course?

What would you like to see changed?

What was the most important thing you learned?

Other comments:

Foundations for Faith

What was the best thing about the course?

What would you like to see changed?

What was the most important thing you learned?

Other comments:

Timely Teaching Tips

What was the best thing about the course?

What would you like to see changed?

What was the most important thing you learned?

Other comments:

Notes

Introduction:
The Challenge before Us

1. Richard Osmer, *A Teachable Spirit: Recovering the Teaching Office in the Church* (Louisville, Ky.: Westminster John Knox Press, 1990), p. 252.
2. Peter L. Benson and Carolyn H. Eklin, *Effective Christian Education: A National Study of Protestant Congregations.* A Report for the Presbyterian Church (U.S.A.) (Minneapolis: Search Institute, 1990), p. 26.
3. Lyle Schaller, *Activating the Passive Church: Diagnosis and Treatment* (Nashville: Abingdon Press, 1981), p. 60.
4. James D. Smart, *The Teaching Ministry of the Church* (Philadelphia: Westminster Press, 1954), p. 70.
5. Locke Bowman, "Analysis and Assessment: The General Protestant Sunday School," in *Renewing the Sunday School and the CCD*, ed. D. Campbell Wyckoff (Birmingham, Ala.: Religious Education Press, 1986), p. 100.
6. Elton Trueblood, quoted in R. Paul Stevens and Phil Collins, *The Equipping Pastor: A Systems Approach to Congregational Leadership* (Washington, D.C.: Alban Institute, 1993), p. 89.

Chapter One:
The Importance of Traditioning

1. W. C. Moragne, "90th Anniversary Address of the Arrival of the French Protestants in South Carolina." Reprinted by the McCormick County Historical Society (McCormick, 1972), p. 43.
2. Maria Harris, *Dance of the Spirit: The Seven Steps of Women's Spirituality* (New York: Bantam, 1989), p. 147.
3. Thomas H. Groome, *Christian Religious Education: Sharing Our Story and Vision* (San Francisco: Harper & Row, 1980) p. 192.
4. James Fowler, *Stages of Faith: The Psychology of Human Development and the Quest for Meaning* (San Francisco: Harper & Row, 1981), p. 136.

Notes

5. Patrick D. Miller, *Deuteronomy: A Bible Commentary for Teaching and Preaching* (Louisville, Ky.: Westminster John Knox Press, 1990), p. 107.

6. Ibid., pp. 107–8.

7. Walter Brueggemann, *The Prophetic Imagination* (Philadelphia: Fortress Press, 1978), p. 66.

Chapter Two:
Called to Teach

1. R. Paul Stevens and Phil Collins, *The Equipping Pastor: A Systems Approach to Congregational Leadership* (Washington, D.C.: Alban Institute, 1993), pp. 138–39.

2. Jim Stockard, "Commissioning the Ministries of the Laity: How It Works and Why It Isn't Being Done," in *The Laity in Ministry: The Whole People of God for the Whole World,* ed. Joanne Owens, George Peck, and John S. Hoffman (Valley Forge, Pa.: Judson Press, 1984), p. 76.

3. George Peck, "The Call to Ministry: Its Meaning and Scope," in *The Laity in Ministry,* ed. Owens, Peck, and Hoffman, pp. 88–89.

4. Ibid.

5. Stevens and Collins, *Equipping Pastor,* p. 135.

6. Norman Shawchuck and Roger Heuser, *Leading the Congregation; Caring for Yourself While Serving the People* (Nashville: Abingdon Press, 1993), p. 147.

7. Frederick Buechner, *Wishful Thinking: A Theological ABC* (Harper San Francisco, 1973), p. 95.

8. For further discussion of "commissioning", see Patrick D. Miller, *Deuteronomy: A Bible Commentary for Teaching and Preaching* (Louisville, Ky.: Westminster John Knox Press, 1990), p. 220.

Chapter Three:
Basic Biblical Background

1. Robin Maas, "The Pastor as Biblical Interpreter and Teacher," in *The Pastor as Religious Educator,* ed. Robert L. Browning (Birmingham, Ala.: Religious Education Press, 1989), pp. 100–101.

2. John Calvin, *Institutes of the Christian Religion,* ed. John T. McNeill, trans. Ford Lewis Battles, The Library of Christian Classics 5, 20, (Philadelphia: Westminster Press, 1960), 1. 6.3, p. 73.

3. See Donald L. Griggs, *Twenty New Ways of Teaching the Bible* (Sacramento, Calif.: Griggs Educational Service, 1977), pp. 19, 20.

4. See Donald L. Griggs. *The Bible from Scratch: An Adult Bible Study Course,* rev. ed. (Sacramento, Calif.: Griggs Educational Service, 1996), p. 23.

5. See D. P. McGeachy III, *Common Sense and the Gospel: Teacher's Book* (Richmond: CLC Press, 1970), p. 21

6. Griggs, *Bible from Scratch,* pp. 57–58.

Notes

Chapter Four:
Foundations for Faith

1. Robert L. Browning, "The Pastor as a Sacramentally Grounded Religious Educator: A Copernican Revolution in the Making," in *The Pastor as Religious Educator,* ed. Robert L. Browning (Birmingham, Ala.: Religious Education Press, 1989), p. 70.

2. Shirley Guthrie, *Christian Doctrine,* rev. ed. (Louisville, Ky.: Westminster John Knox Press, 1994), p. 95.

Chapter Five:
Timely Teaching Tips

1. Parker Palmer, *To Know as We Are Known: A Spirituality of Education* (San Francisco: Harper & Row, 1983), p. 75.

2. See Maria Harris, *Fashion Me a People* (Louisville, Ky.: Westminster John Knox Press, 1989), p. 123.

3. Martha Leypoldt, *Learning Is Change: Adult Education in the Church* (Valley Forge, Pa.: Judson Press, 1971), p. 82.

4. Roberta Hestenes, *Using the Bible in Groups* (Philadelphia: Westminster Press, 1985), p. 40.

5. Donald L. Griggs, *Teaching Teachers to Teach: A Basic Manual for Church Teachers* (Nashville: Abingdon Press, 1980), p. 49.

6. Ibid., p. 51.

7. Palmer, *To Know as We Are Known,* pp. 103–4.

8. Adapted from Hestenes, *Using the Bible in Groups,* pp. 50–60.

Chapter Six:
Equipping the Saints

1. Harris W. Lee, *Effective Church Leadership: A Practical Sourcebook* (Minneapolis: Augsburg Publishing House, 1989), pp. 152–53.

2. Adapted from Mary Alice Douty Edwards, *Leadership Development and the Workers' Conference* (Nashville: Abingdon Press, 1967), p. 64; and Arthur Merrihew Adams, *Effective Leadership for Today's Church* (Philadelphia: Westminster Press, 1978), pp. 71–72.

3. Adapted from Janaan Manternach and Carl J. Pfeiffer, *Creative Catechist: A Comprehensive, Illustrated Guide for Training Religion Teachers* (Mystic, Conn.: Twenty-third Publications, 1991), p. 148.

4. Adapted from Edwards, *Leadership Development,* pp. 65–66.

Printed in the United States
1390900002BA/23-90